The
Sixties

The Long Decade
1954 - 1974

Clemson University Emeritus College

Copyright 2025

ISBN: 979-8-218-84465-3

Cover:
Montage comprising images found within the text.

Introduction

The essays in this book were written by members of Clemson University's Emeritus College Memoir Group. The group began as an online Zoom activity in the spring of 2021 at the height of the Covid epidemic and was initiated by Emeritus College Director Debra Jackson and Emeritus member Marty Duckenfield. Looking back, Covid may have brought us together online, but other considerations have kept us working collaboratively for four and a half years, and we are still going strong. Our reasons for writing grew out of lively discussions online among people who had important things to say. The engaging stories in this book are the result of that process. Fortuitously, some members in the group had experience editing and publishing memoirs, which led naturally to the creation of the book.

The memoir group has numbered between twelve to eighteen, including many who've remained steady participants. The experiences of these writers, retired staff and faculty from Clemson University, are varied. The writers were born and grew up in various places: farming communities (Georgia, Kansas, South Carolina); Smalltown, USA (South Carolina, Georgia, Michigan, New York), and urban and suburban environments (Charlotte, NC; Indianapolis, IN; Jersey City, NJ; NYC; Barranquilla, Colombia). Their academic disciplines include Agronomy and Soils, Architecture, Education, English, Food Science,

Mechanical Engineering, Nursing, Political Science, and Spanish.

Why memoirs? Retired people are drawn to the genre of memoir, like a moth to flame. That's not hard to figure. At this time in life, we seek to understand how events of our past have influenced our lives. During our careers we were busy seeking education, maintaining relationships, raising families, teaching, researching, and collaborating with colleagues and students along the way. In the process, we had little time to examine the sum total of past experience and make sense of it. Now it's time.

Why the Sixties? Just as our Zoom discussions were fertile soil for writing prompts to sprout in, the writing that resulted was fertile soil for Sixties themes to grow in. We did not start with someone saying, "Hey, let's write a book about the Sixties!" Rather, after years of writing together, someone observed, "You know, we've written a lot about the Sixties." That observation surprised us at first, but it shouldn't have. As retired people of "a certain age" who spent their developmental years living through a tumultuous and transformative decade, it seems natural to look back to that period in our lives and make sense of it. Consequently, this book raises issues from the Sixties that were vital concerns to the writers. The stories herein reflect how the Sixties forced Americans to make decisions and choices that led to sometimes difficult, sometimes rewarding, yet always interesting lives.

The book is divided into themes: "The Kennedy Era," "Civil Rights, "The Space Race," "Vietnam," "You've Come a Long Way" (Women's Rights), and "Reflections (miscellany), a few of the important issues of the Sixties. All the stories in "The Kennedy Era" focus on the effects of the assassination of JFK on the writer, an event about which for decades every American, even those who were children at the time, could remember where he or she was on

November 22, 1963. Clementina E. Adams's story, "John F. Kennedy from a Colombian Perspective," takes a broader view of the event, recalling JFK as a beloved American president who appealed to the humanitarian idealism inherent in the people of many nations.

Although the Civil Rights Movement began in earnest in the Fifties, most people recognize it was not truly enacted until the Sixties, notably with LBJ's signing of the Civil Rights Act of 1964 and the Voting Rights Act of 1965. Many would say the movement has not yet completed its mission. The book's section, "Civil Rights," focuses on the movement's effect on public spaces, public school classrooms, and public work environments. Victoria Ridgeway Gillis's memoir, "Civil Rights Become Real," reminds us of challenges public school teachers faced when the 1954 *Brown v. Board of Education* Supreme Court Decision was finally imposed on schools in the late Sixties and early Seventies.

Like JFK's assassination, another Sixties event about which many people recall vividly where they were at that moment was the July 1969, American moon landing and Neil Armstrong's words as he stepped off the ladder of the Apollo Lunar Module onto the moon. Most of us shared a sense of awe and pride then, although some skeptics swore that the landing was staged in a remote part of the Arizona desert (some still believe it). I imagine in 1961 when Kennedy predicted the event and his goal to accomplish it by the end of the Sixties many Americans thought he was dreaming or deranged, but if it was a dream, it came true to the astonishment of all nations. Don Collins narrates an amusing story of his Aunt Peggy and how her name ended up stitched into the hem of the American flag that was planted on the moon's surface on that first lunar visit.

The "Vietnam" section is the longest in the book, perhaps because it most affected the writers personally. In this section you'll find two compelling stories of men who enlisted. Stephen H. Wainscott's memoir, "On the Catawba River," recounts his gut-wrenching moral decision to enlist in the U.S. Army. Writer Delores (Dee) Stegelin's memoir, "Growing Through the Sixties," tells the story of her young husband's enlistment in the Air Force while still a student at Kansas State University, and their tragic experience of his being shot down over Vietnam (he was injured, rescued, and survived).

This book would not be complete without a section on women's rights, aptly titled "You've Come A Long Way." More than half of the book's contributors are successful women having enjoyed outstanding careers at Clemson University. I know all of them would say they have benefitted from the transformation of women's roles in society that developed in the Sixties; they not only benefitted from it but contributed to it. Theirs are stories of confidence, courage, and conviction, as all stories about women's rights are, and they are fascinating: women in the professions, athletics, and academia, all independent women and women in pants (how shocking!) Readers will enjoy Jim Palmer's retelling of the ludicrous obstacles his wife faced in the newspaper industry on her way to becoming a nationally known and syndicated political cartoonist. Jim's story is humorously delivered but no laughing matter.

In the last section, "Reflections," the writers touch on subjects tangentially related to the other sections but all having to do with moments of change: cultural reforms, political awakenings, Watergate, communal living arrangements, youthful spontaneity, music, fashion, and life in the Sixties.

Finally, there is the book's subtitle that denotes the Sixties as *"The Long Decade: 1954-1974,"* which we thought might puzzle a few readers. We refer to each distinctive period in our relatively recent history by a descriptive nickname—Roaring Twenties, Depression Era, War Years, Post-War Boom, Turbulent Sixties, and Swinging Seventies. I'm not sure about the Eighties, Nineties, and 2000s because I have not caught up to them yet. But each period had its roots in a previous decades and stretched its tentacles into the next ones. Such is the case of the Sixties. We would not have had the Sixties we had, if not for *Brown v. Board of Education* in 1954. And the street and campus protestors of the Sixties did not magically disappear in 1970; they helped bring about the end of the Vietnam War and Nixon's resignation in 1975. And there are many more such connections between the Fifties, Sixties, and Seventies. Significant changes are not dictated by prescribed time periods but by the people who live through those times.

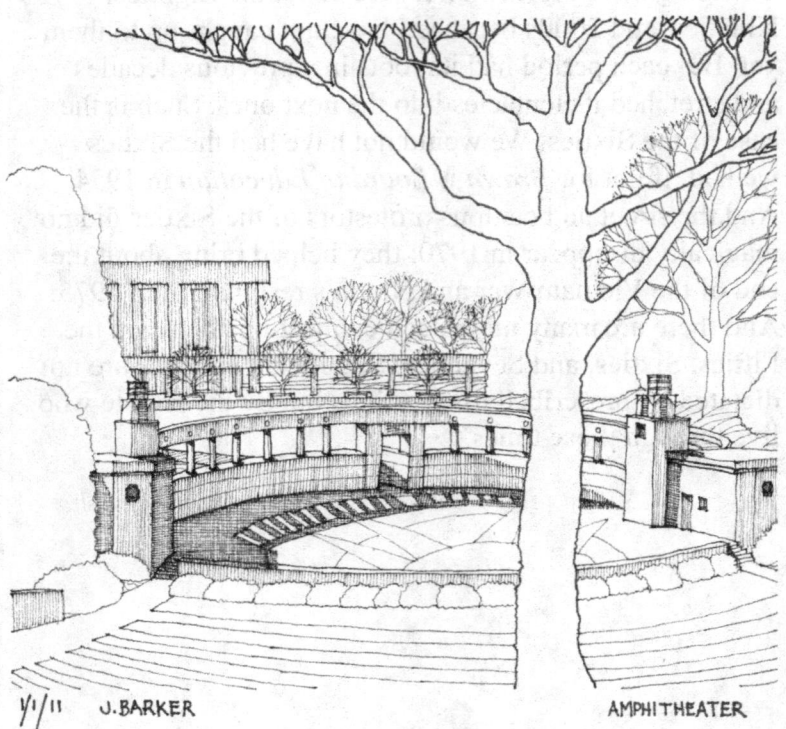

J.BARKER   AMPHITHEATER

Amphitheater, Reflection Pond, and R.M. Cooper Library
Clemson University campus

With permission of the artist, Clemson President Emeritus James F. Barker

Table of Contents

Civil Rights

The Space Race

Vietnam

Contents

Reflections

Contributors

The Kennedy Era

Lyndon B. Johnson takes the oath of office aboard Air Force One, November 22, 1963.

Lyndon B. Johnson Library Photo by Cecil Stoughton

Public domain, via Wikimedia Commons:
https://commons.wikimedia.org/wiki/File:Lyndon_B._Johnson_taking_the_oath_of_office,_November_1963.jpg

Accessed August 23, 2025

Premonition

Susan Hilligoss

I had gone to the school library and was reading *Oliver Twist* when the public address system came on. I don't know who made the announcement or remember what was said. A sad novel, then a shocking announcement. The mostly empty library was still. I stared at the brown speaker box high on the wall whence the voice came. But there was no other sound. I kept reading, now and then looking up through the massive windows on one side of the room to the barren trees and the dreary, drizzly midwestern sky. I had been glad to be away from my tenth-grade English class, a rare opportunity to avoid communal boredom while an oblivious teacher droned on. The rest of the school day left no mark.

At home there was routine. A dog to walk, a baby brother to tend to, dinner preparations. We watched the news on television in the downstairs family room. It was where I had watched my first political conventions and presidential debates three years before. My father's mother, Nonie, had been staying with us in 1960. She watched all of the election news, and I watched with her. Nonie despised the Kennedys, and so did my father. She did not live to see the assassination.

So, on November 22, 1963, and for days after, the downstairs TV again became the center of attention. It was one thing to hate the government in power, and another to change it by violence.

My father had flown to Dallas for a sales meeting just the week before. He had never been to Texas. He came back shocked by the casual presence of guns everywhere. I can still see the look in his eyes when he returned. When I think of JFK's assassination, mixed in with the blizzard of gruesome, poignant images of our collective memory, I also see my father's pale blue eyes with fear in them.

Sad Reminders: Kennedy's Assassination and Funeral

Victoria Ridgeway Gillis

For each generation, at least one major event marks the generation forever. For Baby Boomers, one date to make an indelible mark was November 22, 1963. I was a senior in high school. On that afternoon in November, our principal interrupted our physics class with an announcement that President Kennedy had been assassinated in Dallas, Texas; he cried as he made the announcement. Numb and moving like an automaton, I gathered my books when the bell rang and headed for band, my last class of the day.

Our band teacher was an ostrich-like man, slim to the point of seeming malnutrition, with large eyes and hair combed over a balding head, who came to us from Mississippi. He was not well-liked by students. As we entered the band room, stunned into silence, tears streaming down our faces, his reaction was swift and brutal, "I'm glad the SOB is dead." At that remark my dislike of him bloomed into a loathing that never abated. School was dismissed, and I walked home to begin a vigil in front of the television.

My father had died the year before. The constant beating of drums as JFK's body was carried through the streets of Washington, DC, the young widow with her two small children, John-John saluting his father's caisson as it passed by: these sounds and images were reminders of the funeral I had attended not that long ago for my own father. President Kennedy's funeral was held on my 17th birthday. There was no cake, or presents, or any celebration of my birthday that year. Just the sound of drums and the images of stunned people, and the overwhelming sadness and despair that permeated my family at that time.

The World Came to a Stop

Marty Duckenfield

I had been a freshman at a small co-ed college in Maine for just two months, six hours by car from my hometown of Hartsdale, New York. At Bates College, I found a new home in my dormitory, Mitchell House, an old three-story house right down the street from the quad. With just 21 women in that dorm, freshmen through juniors, we would all come to know each other well, and some lifelong friendships began there. On that day, November 22, 1963, just a week before Thanksgiving, Mitchell House's small size afforded us a place of comfort where we were to bond tightly over an unexpected national tragedy.

I was in the dormitory lounge, about to go to class, when the first news arrived from Shirley Murphy, whose room was just across the entry hall. She came into the lounge, having just had a shower, wearing a towel wrapped around her head and a stricken look on her face. "The president has been shot!" Just like that. She had heard it on her radio. No more information other than "stay tuned," so we all left in a bewildered state to our one o'clock class.

When I got to my freshman English class, our professor, Mr. Nelson, had not yet arrived. Everyone was talking with concern about the news of President Kennedy. Suddenly Mr. Nelson burst through the open door, and this normally calm man was visibly distraught. He had never burst into the classroom; he had never run his hand through his mop of sandy blond hair. But this day he did both. Did we have a class? I cannot recall, but I do recall his great distress. We all remained in the dark as to what was to come.

If we had the class, it was after two when it let out. Everyone on campus was rushing back to places where they had friends or dormmates and a radio. We had to find out whether the president was okay.

Of course, he was not. The finality of the news came very soon after the news of the shooting, and it was shocking and sobering.

Across the street from Mitchell House was the Hobby Shop, where we did our laundry downstairs, but upstairs was a soda fountain with a TV mounted on the far wall. Going over there to watch the news, some of the sophomores had found out that this major historic news event and the planned events to come were to be televised live over the weekend and through the funeral on Monday. Someone got out the Yellow Pages and found a place where we could rent a TV for the three days, and we got one delivered by Saturday morning. The lounge in Mitchell House was really two rooms with sitting areas but enough floor space to seat others, and most of us gravitated there to watch the constant broadcast. The TV showed us the unfolding story, including the capture and shooting of Lee Harvey Oswald, totally absorbing us for hours on end. The world came to a stop to collectively mourn. Classes were cancelled for Monday.

For nearly every moment of those three days, I was very quiet and withdrawn. Like most of the other girls, I was focused on what we saw and heard on that black and white screen. Strong, unfamiliar emotions engulfed all of us— sadness, confusion, worry. I had some feelings of internal discomfort as well: I was dealing with a case of cognitive dissonance.

Back home in my family household, the domain of my strongly Republican father, there might have been shock, but had there been any mourning at the level I was experiencing? As an 18-year-old far from home at such a moment, I wondered, "How am I supposed to feel?" I was swept away by not only my own raw emotions but also those of the other girls—especially seeing the images that centered on Jackie and her two young children, which were heartbreaking. But my father hated Kennedy, and somehow this confused me. I had always believed him to be right, but I never asked him about this. I either didn't want to know, or I feared I would be even more confused no matter what he said. Kennedy's assassination was the beginning of a crack in the family ecosystem I had been born into and believed in. And a different view of the world started to appear.

Walter Cronkite, broadcast journalist during the presidential debate between Gerald Ford and Jimmy Carter,

September 23, 1976

A Real-Life Horror Story

Debra Broadwell Jackson

November 22, 1963, was a Friday, and my brother Michael's 17th birthday. I had just turned 14. John Kennedy's assassination was a horrific event, and I remember clearly the day. I was in ninth-grade English class when the announcement was made. I think everyone was shocked, but I did not know exactly what his death meant or how Kennedy's death would affect me personally. My teacher was extremely upset but did not say much. I do not remember classes after the announcement. The bus ride home was uneventful, and no one was talking about Kennedy's death. As always, I was carrying textbooks, notebooks, and lists of homework assignments, as I did on any Friday afternoon.

My brother was inconsolable that evening and glued to the TV coverage. He and my mother loved Kennedy and his wife. I went to a birthday party sleepover for a friend that night. There were fifteen girls at the party, and if we mentioned Kennedy at all, it was to lament that every television channel was non-stop on the coverage of the assassination. We finally found a horror movie to watch, ate popcorn, and talked all night.

This was the first time that I experienced TV coverage of an event that was non-stop. Two days later, I was watching the TV coverage when Lee Harvey Oswald was killed. In some ways, this was more disturbing for me because it was live. I saw a person killed. I saw the arrest of Jack Ruby. I kept wondering how Ruby could have been in the hallway with a gun. It was full of policemen and reporters; how could he have shot Oswald?

The Kennedy funeral on November 25 had a powerful impact on me—seeing Jacqueline and her children and realizing that they would never see their father again. Little John was so young; would he have any memories of his dad? I watched the funeral with my brother while our parents worked.

Was I afraid? No. Nothing stopped. We visited our family for Thanksgiving on November 28th, six days after the death of Kennedy. My family talked about the assassination and the funeral, and everyone was horrified that the shooting occurred. My aunt and uncle lived in the Dallas area at the time and were with us for Thanksgiving. The next week we were back at school, getting ready for the holidays. Did the world change? Most likely. But not in my small, isolated 14-year-old world.

Much later I realized the significance of what happened on that day. It took time for the conspiratory theories and the Zapruder movie to be released and analyzed over and over. No one seemed to believe the official reports. I remember reading that Kennedy's brain had been discarded at the autopsy (at fourteen and now, 62 years later, I have no idea if this was true), but all the crime novels I read led me to believe it was essential to trace the path of the bullet through a body. My unhealthy reading habits were well known by my parents, and conspiratory theories make great novels. One of my all-time favorite books is Stephen King's *11/22/63*. My imagination works with King's stories; the imagery his words create is vivid and disturbing. The main character, Jake, an English teacher, travels back and forth in time to try and prevent Kennedy's assassination. Every time Jake goes through the time portal, he changes the past and the future, but he keeps trying. How would America and the world have been different if Kennedy had lived? King's imaginative book gives a glimpse into possibilities. But we will never know.

John F. Kennedy

Library of Congress Prints and Photographs Division
Washington, D.C. 20540 USA
https://www.loc.gov/resource/cph.3a53304/
Accessed September 22, 2025

The Kennedy Assassination from a Fresh-Out-of-the-Military Mindset

Don Collins

On 31 August 63, I was released from active duty with the United States Air Force. The early separation from active duty was granted to facilitate my post-Labor Day enrollment in Clemson University as a Bachelor of Architecture major. Despite having earned 27 hours of college credit from Furman University while stationed at Donaldson Air Force Base south of Greenville, SC, I was still classified as a freshman. Being married and four years older than my classmates, I was, I like to think, more mature than many. I was certainly serious about my studies and did not like distractions.

Arriving in the design studio on that fateful afternoon day of 22 Nov 63, we were told that all first-year students were to go the auditorium—that Dean McClure wanted to speak to the class. After we were all seated, well most of the 100 students in first-year studio, Dean McClure came into the room, spoke quietly to our faculty members, and walked to the lectern at the front of the room. It was obvious that he was upset and shaken about something. I had only seen him a few times in the hallways, but I knew something was amiss.

He began to address us by speaking about the assigned project we were working on in the studio and our duty to do the best with the assignment, our duty to be inventive and creative in our choice of materials to use in its execution. But he then began speaking about professional integrity and honesty. This was a prelude to his revelation that one of my less mature classmates had appropriated—no, stolen—a wooden soft drink crate from outside a country store just over the county line to use as part of his solution to the assignment. I remember thinking his obvious emotional stress seemed grossly exaggerated over a petty-theft incident and wondering why he was taking it so personally. With a statement that theft would not be tolerated in Lee Hall, he dismissed us and ordered us back to our studio.

McClure never mentioned that John F. Kennedy, 35th President of the United States and Commander-in-Chief of United States Armed Forces, had been shot in Dallas. Nor did he even suggest we should return to our studios and turn on a radio.

I was sitting near the back of the auditorium close to the door. I bounded up the stairs two at a time to get back to my desk to make up for time lost on my project. As I flung open the door to the studio at the top of the stairs, I was met by one of the less mature students who had skipped the mandatory briefing. His eyes were wide as he shouted, "President Kennedy has been shot." I pushed him aside saying, "Oh get out of here," for he was one of the few students who had mouthed anti-Kennedy statements earlier that fall. He continued saying, "I'm not joking, man, listen to the radio." Would this lead to war?

Many times, thinking about that moment when I learned of Kennedy's assassination and the emotions I experienced, I have come to understand how my parents must have felt on 7 Dec 41, the date forces of Japan attacked American naval vessels and army installations in and around Pearl Harbor. World War II began for the United States with the Japanese attack. People's lives changed forever. I grew up hearing people occasionally ask, "Where were you when you heard the news about Pearl Harbor?"

I knew immediately on hearing about President Kennedy's assassination that fall afternoon how quickly evolving events and national actions and reaction could sweep me up in any outcome with just one telegram. In the event of a national emergency, I was still subject to recall from "Inactive Reserve" status by the United States Air Force until 10 Jan 66. A terrible dread nearly overwhelmed me knowing this one event could change my life forever. My college journey could be over before it barely began.

I had become an ardent Kennedy fan watching his performance during the Kennedy-Nixon debates during the campaign. My first presidential ballot was cast voting for Kennedy. My ardor grew stronger watching his inaugural address. Who could not forget and be inspired by "Ask not what your country can do for you—ask what you can do for your country." Wow!

Later in his presidency, Kennedy's speech in West Berlin at the Wall that divided the city, when he said to the people of Berlin, "Ich bin ein Berliner" (I am also a citizen of Berlin) was equally inspiring. That West Berlin speech was especially meaningful for me, for I, too, had had a responsibility for the citizens of Berlin as a very large part of my military service.

During the Cold War, the Soviet Union on 24 Jun 48 blocked all land access to West Berlin to get the United States, France and Great Britain to withdraw from their administrative areas of Berlin, located deep inside Soviet administered East Germany. The Soviet Union was miffed because the United States, Great Britain, and France had agreed to consolidate their zones in West Germany and West Berlin, turning them over to German administration, with a seat of government in Bonn.

The West countered the land blockade with a massive airlift to resupply everything needed by western forces and the citizens of Berlin living in the western sectors. The "Berlin Airlift" as it was known, lasted until 12 May 49 when the Soviets relented and removed the blockades.

But the possibility of a new blockade was always there. The USAF's Military Airlift Command constantly trained crews to fly through the three established air corridors into the three airfields located in the western sectors of Berlin. The Berlin Corridor flight training was done in a C-124 Globemaster cargo plane flight simulator. My job at Donaldson was to brief the pilots, co-pilots, and flight engineers before the flight, on navigation aids available to use during the mission and be one of three people operating the simulator during the mission.

When President Kennedy ordered the naval blockade of Cuba during the Cuban Missile Crisis, the simulator school operated around the clock because the U.S. expected the Soviets to establish a countermeasure by once again blocking land access to Berlin. Thankfully, it never happened.

But the possibility existed that the assassination of Kennedy was in some way related to his audacity in ordering the blockade of Cuba. Not only was I now dealing with the grief from the death of my hero President, but also the realization that World War III could be upon us. My academic journey could be delayed, or perhaps over, before it barely got started.

What is or will be your date to remember where you were when you first learned that history-in-the-making was about to alter your life?

John F. Kennedy from a Colombian Perspective

Clementina E. Adams

The Kennedy family was known throughout Colombia and other Latin American countries. President Kennedy was loved and admired everywhere in my country. The myth of Camelot, with a handsome President, a beautiful wife and lovely young and innocent children was fascinating. President Kennedy had visited many countries in Latin America. On his visit to Colombia, President Kennedy provided aid to our country, not only by motivating our president to start school cafeterias for students but also by assisting in the building of top-quality cafeterias for elementary and high schools. Indeed, he provided some of the equipment required to make the cafeterias a reality. The goal was to assist in the provision of good nutrition for our school children. It was the beginning of a great project that still continues in Colombia. When a new suburb was built in Bogotá, our capital city, it was named after President Kennedy. We were especially thankful and impressed by the way he managed the Cuban Missile Crisis.

One night in Barranquilla we watched a film that was shown in a public plaza. The film showed President

Kennedy delivering a discourse in Costa Rica about the problem of rodents and insects in that region and how to control them. In the same film he explained how those insects transmitted bacteria and infections. He also provided the knowledge and chemicals to control those pests. The presentation was done in such a vivid manner that even today I cannot tolerate the thought of a roach.

November 22, 1963, is one of the saddest days in my memory. I came home from school and found my family seated around the television in complete silence; I sat down and joined them. The news was shocking and sad; tears came to my eyes as I wondered how humanity could be so cruel as to put such a tragic end to the life of a beloved humanitarian and president. There were reports in the newspapers and on TV of women crying in the streets, and the whole country was at a standstill with people sitting in front of their TVs and wondering how it could have happened. There were flowers and offerings, moments of silence and prayers, accompanied by the lighting of candles. All the states in Colombia flew our National Flag at half-mast, and several nationwide moments of silence were observed in President Kennedy's honor.

Kennedy's death brought sad memories to my father. The year 1963 in Barranquilla was a peaceful and happy time nationwide; but my father told us that it had not always been so because there had been a dark period in the past. My father sat among his seven children and began to tell us a story. It was similar in some respects to Kennedy's tragic death.

According to my father, in 1948, an election year, a candidate named Jorge Eliezer Gaitan was the people's candidate. He was intelligent, charismatic, and visionary. Gaitan was shot and killed while walking on a street with a multitude of followers. That was the beginning of a period of violence in Colombia that lasted almost ten years.

On the day of the assassination of Gaitan, my father was driving back home when he saw people running around with machetes and clubs, and they appeared out of control. A group of people began stopping vehicles on the street to ask a simple question, "Are you Liberal [democrat] or Conservador [republican]?" According to one's answer one would be killed or allowed to drive away. When they came to my father, he prayed to God that he could survive and return home to his family; at the same time my mother, unaware of the situation, was lighting a candle and praying for my father's safety. Facing the question, my father hesitated for one second and decided to be truthful. So, he replied, "I am a Liberal" and waited for his fate. Fortunately, that group was from the Liberal party and my father's life was spared.

During my first year at Florida State University in Tallahassee in 1973, I became better acquainted with the life and works of President Kennedy and learned more details about his tragic death. Later, with my husband, I visited his grave and saw the eternal flame burning in his honor. I reflected on such a special person who was taken away in such a sudden and tragic way.

It is interesting and puzzling that such a historic and notorious assassination is still fraught with speculations and conspiracy theories even today, sixty-two years later. During my year of study at FSU in Florida, I watched several documentaries about the assassination of Robert Kennedy, another intelligent and charismatic man, and a presidential candidate. It is no wonder that after John and Robert Kennedy's deaths, people everywhere in the world became even more interested in the lives and activities of the Kennedy clan.

Signature of John F Kennedy

Image traced from original, August 28, 2009

Public domain via "Wikimedia Commons."

https://commons.wikimedia.org/wiki/File:John_F_Kennedy_Signature_2.svg#/
media/File:John_F_Kennedy_Signature_2.svg

Accessed October 28, 2025

From Tranquility to Harsh Reality: The Impact of the Kennedy Assassination

Dolores (Dee) Stegelin

Prelude to the Sixties—Growing Up in Rural
Kansas. Of the seven plus decades that I have lived,
the Sixties were the most impactful. The assassination of
JFK in November of 1963 marked the first real trauma
that I experienced. Having grown up on a dairy farm in
north central Kansas, my childhood consisted of long days
outdoors; taking care of baby calves, lambs, and puppies;
and helping with the chores that come with life on a farm.
In retrospect, my childhood was somewhat sheltered—a
stable family with four children, a mom who loved to be
a homemaker, and an energetic dairy farmer father who
provided a quiet, steady sense of security for our family.
Our simple life was marked by routines of assuming
responsibilities at young ages and developing a love of the
outdoors, the animals, and the land that transitioned through
the seasons. I loved the farm—the rhythms of life were
reassuring—and as I grew older, I came to truly appreciate

that my childhood provided and prepared me for the years ahead.

The Memorable Moments of November 22, 1963. In the Fall of 1963, I was a sophomore in a consolidated rural high school of 500 students in Chapman, Kansas, an excellent high school with dedicated and knowledgeable teachers. Most of us took small buses from our farms to a central site, and then we transferred to a larger school bus; the total trip took about 45 minutes. After eight years of schooling in a small rural school of twenty students, the transition to high school was both exhilarating and, at times, intimidating.

I was settled into my sophomore year when, on that infamous November 22nd, I was standing at the checkout area of the high school library, waiting my turn to process the books I was eager to read. It was just after lunch, around 1:20 pm CST, and all was quiet in the peaceful library environs.

Then there was a loud "click," and the school intercom system came on with a radio announcement: President Kennedy had been shot and had died. Time stood still for a moment, and I felt disoriented—surely this could not be true! It took me a while to accept and believe what I had just heard.

The next four days were a blur. Our black and white TV in the living room of our house was on constantly, and I was glued to the images that were being televised. It seemed surreal, and I felt if I just watched the TV, it might all end and go away. But, of course, that didn't happen. The images from Dallas, the replaying of JFK's car slowly meandering through the city streets, the high-rise building from which the shooter mounted his terror, the unforgettable pictures of Jackie and her pink, stained suit, soaked with her husband's blood, the president slumped over in the car, and the many,

many officers moving through the streets and calming the shocked and traumatized people along the parade route. Concerned that I might be absorbing too much from these images, my father suggested we turn off the TV for a while—but we didn't. The black and white images were riveting: the horse-drawn carriage with the president's casket, Jackie and her two tiny children, John-John's sweet attentive salute to his father's entourage and casket, and the image of Jackie in black shroud, gracefully suffering her own private trauma, even as she helped to transfer power to Lyndon Johnson.

When the dust settled on that event, I believe I emerged a different person. To this day, over sixty years later, that day remains one of the most memorable moments of my life. The magnitude of the event intruding into my relatively sheltered young life rocked my world view. For me, this event contributed to a more cautious perspective on life. Overnight I felt changed from a trusting, sheltered, and hopeful teenager to a more guarded, wary, and perceptive pre-adult. Looking back, I wonder if witnessing the Kennedy Assassination in 1963—the first major death that I had experienced—may have helped to prepare me to cope with the unexpected loss of my father the next year. The grief I shared with all Americans at Kennedy's death may have been a foreshadowing of the feelings of personal loss I would experience at my father's passing. To this day, November 22, 1963, remains one of the most existential, turning point days of my 70-plus years of life.

My Father and the President

Chris Benson

I n the fall of 1963, I turned seven years old in the second
grade at St. Agnes Parochial School in West Chester,
Pennsylvania. On the 22nd of November, I happened to
be out of school with a mild fever. Since my mother, a
young widow, worked daily at a law office, she dropped me
off that day at Mrs. Anderson's house across the country
road we lived on. Mrs. Anderson lived in a dilapidated
manor situated on many acres of neglected farmland.
Mr. Anderson had died long before I was born, and the
Andersons' adult children had long since left the farm to
pursue their own fortunes. In her late sixties, Mrs. Anderson
dressed like a farm woman from another time; she wore
ankle-length, roomy skirts and long-sleeved white blouses
with buttoned-up high collars; she rolled up her sleeves
when she worked in her flower gardens, the only part of the
extensive farm that she kept up. She was a kind woman,
but even at seven years old I knew she was a no-nonsense
person, and I minded my Ps & Qs around her.

After Ma dropped me off that day, I immediately began
to feel better. By midmorning, my slight fever was all but
gone, and I busied myself in the rooms of Mrs. Anderson's
large two-story house with the few toys I'd brought to pass
the day: a spongy rubber ball, a cowboy cap gun without

any caps, and an Etch-a-Sketch. I was fiddling with the Etch-a-Sketch in the high-ceilinged parlor that afternoon when I heard Mrs. Anderson gasp and cry, "Oh, my God!"

I ran with my Etch-a-Sketch into the adjacent den where she was standing in front of a black and white television. A man on TV was explaining something bad had happened. I didn't know what he was talking about, but he looked like he was about to cry. Then Mrs. Anderson said to herself in disbelief, "They've shot the President! They've shot the President!" I knew the President was somebody important.

I sat on the sofa and watched Mrs. Anderson. She paid no attention to me, and I knew not to interrupt her as she watched the images on the TV. We sat there for a long time, watching men holding microphones saying the same things:

"We are waiting to hear from the surgeons who operated on President Kennedy."

"Mrs. Kennedy was not injured."

"Texas Governor Connally was seriously injured and is in the same hospital as the President."

Though the TV bored me, Mrs. Anderson's rapt attention to the little black and white images fascinated me.

Eventually, Mrs. Anderson left the room, came back in a moment, and turned off the TV. In her hand was a long rosary with large black beads, the longest one I'd ever seen that wasn't hanging from the waist of a nun. Mrs. Anderson sat next to me on the sofa. She looked at my face for a long time, like she was looking for something, and finally said, "Chris, I want you to pray for President Kennedy with me." She bowed her head and started off with the "Apostles Creed," which I was only just beginning to learn. I watched her lips like I watched the lips of Sister Saint Kevin, my teacher, and tried to say the right words. When she got to the "Our Fathers" and "Hail, Marys," which I knew backwards and forwards, I prayed hard for the President.

It took a long time to say the whole rosary. I stopped concentrating and raised my head to take peeks at Mrs. Anderson's face, which looked stern. I forgot about the President and said the prayers to my father, like my mother had taught me. She always reminded me, "Pray to Daddy in heaven." Before we finished, I remembered the President and said the prayers for him and my father.

When we were done, Mrs. Anderson leaned against the back of the sofa and breathed a big sigh of relief like she'd just dropped something heavy off her shoulders. She was calm. She wasn't smiling but her face wasn't stern anymore. We sat a while not talking, until I felt it was okay to get off the sofa and go back to my Etch-a-Sketch. But before I could move, Mrs. Anderson grabbed my hand and said, "Stay here, Chris." I sat back down on the sofa. After a while, she turned the TV on again, and I fiddled away the rest of the afternoon beside her, playing with the Etch-a-Sketch. She kept saying to herself, "I can't believe it. The poor woman and her children!"

Ma came home early that day. I thought she came home early because I was sick. But she said everybody at work went home early. By then I knew the President was somebody important. And he had a son who was younger than me. The boy's name was John. My father's middle name was John. My father was dead and in heaven, and now that boy's father was in heaven, too. It was a sad day, but I was glad his father and mine, too, were in heaven. And I hoped they knew each other there. For a long time after, I prayed to the two of them, my father and the President.

Civil Rights

Civil Rights March on Washington, D.C. / [WKL], August 28,, 1963.

Leffler, Warren K., photographer

Accessed August 23, 2025

Encounters with "Segregation"

Stephen H. Wainscott

The Parking Lot. For the first half of his career, my
father was a chemist with DuPont. In 1952, he moved
into sales and was transferred to Charlotte, NC. There were
many mornings when he would get in his company car at
the same time my brother and I would leave the house to
catch the school bus. Normally, he would be on the road
for an entire week, calling on accounts throughout North
Carolina and South Carolina. However, there were also
times when he would work out of his home office, doing
paperwork or calling accounts by phone.

One day, when I was nine or ten, Dad asked if I would
like to go with him to downtown Charlotte while he would
meet with the managers of stores that carried DuPont
automotive products. He wanted me to know what his
world of work was like. I found the prospect boring, but I
didn't want to disappoint him.

As I expected, I was bored, and the visits seemed to last
forever. Finally, we left and returned to the car, which Dad
had parked in a large lot behind Efird's Department Store.
As we approached the car, a large commotion was going
on. A crowd of white people was cursing, screaming, and

using the n-word. Making our way through the crowd, we saw many of them spitting on and kicking a terrified Black woman who was sobbing. Her underwear was down around her ankles. I noticed a pool of liquid on the pavement.

Dad took charge of the situation and dispersed the crowd. Through her tears, the woman apologized. I wondered for what. She thanked Dad and proceeded to explain that she had been shopping in Efird's when she had the urge to use the restroom, only to find that the one for "colored" women was out of order. She knew that entering the restroom for "white women" was forbidden, as were the ones for men, white or colored.

Faced with this dilemma, she proceeded to the crowded parking lot where she felt safe that she could relieve herself between two cars and not be spotted. Dad put his jacket over her so that she could pull up her underwear. He asked if she needed anything else. She said no, again thanked Dad, and walked away, still sobbing.

On the drive home, Dad didn't speak a word, but I could tell that he was upset. I knew he was not given to displays of emotion; he did his best to hold them in. When we went in the house, Dad asked me to go to another room while he talked with my mother about the incident. I couldn't make out their conversation, but I heard him say, "What's wrong with these people?"

The Backstory, Alma. In my first semester at Clemson, I taught three sections of an introductory course on American government and politics. In the unit on civil rights, I started by explaining the Supreme Court's 1896 ruling in the case of *Plessy v. Ferguson* in which the Court validated racial segregation on the principle of "separate but equal." From there, I traced the history of Court decisions through the 20th century up to 1954 when the Court overturned Plessy and ruled that segregated schools were inherently unequal, and that desegregation was to proceed with "all deliberate speed."

Without raising his hand, a student in the back of the room blurted out, "What's so bad about separate but equal? Sounds like a good idea to me." It took me awhile to collect myself and think about how to respond. Finally, I told the following story.

Like most white middle-class families in suburban Charlotte, we had a "colored maid." Her name was Alma. One day in 1962, I came home from school to find Alma in a frantic state. She explained that her husband James could not bring their three sons home from school because his truck had broken down. Alma asked if I would drive her to the school to pick them up. "Alma," I asked, "why don't they take the school bus home?" She replied, "J.H. Gunn School doesn't have school buses. You need to take me there."

At the time, I had had my driver's license only a couple of months, and my parents were reluctant to let me take the family car on my own. But seeing that Alma was in a predicament, we hopped in the 1950 Chevy and went to the school which was several miles out in the country in a red dirt field with hardly any grass and no trees. When we entered the school, Alma said she would go down the hall to the right and pick up her ninth-grade son James Jr., while I would go down the hall to the left and get eighth-grade Edison and sixth-grade Dewey.

As I got to the end of the hall, I found Edison and Dewey in the same classroom. I was confused, until the teacher explained that she taught sixth, seventh, and eighth grades together. The desks were cracked with many having a leg missing. The slate blackboard was cracked and had large pieces missing. I noticed some of the textbooks. Most had covers torn off and pages missing. I recognized them; they were books I'd had in the fourth and fifth grades.

After picking up the boys, I looked around the school. There was no cafeteria. No playground with swings and sliding boards. No ball fields, no gym, no athletic teams, no school band. Just a stark two-story brick building out in the middle of nowhere.

After telling this story, I addressed the student, "So, what was your question?"

U.S. Marshals with young Ruby Bridges on school steps, November 1960

Failing Gus Roberts

Don Collins

On a Wednesday, September 4th, 1957, I began my junior year of high school. It was three years after the United States Supreme Court, in *Brown v. Board of Education*, had ruled that "separate but equal" schools based on race were inherently not equal and therefore the practice of segregated schools by race must end. On that early September Wednesday, four Black students enrolled at Charlotte's previously all-white high schools. Central High, my school, a mile from the city center, was one of them. Central, just across Little Sugar Creek from a Black neighborhood that roughly occupied the creek's floodplain, enrolled only one Black student—a 16-year-old skinny kid by the name of Gus Roberts.

As I was getting into my car to drive to school that day, my father said to me, "There may be trouble at your school today. Stay away from the main entrance. I want you go in one of the back entrances and go straight to your homeroom. Whatever happens inside or outside the building, I want you to stay clear of it. Do you understand me?" I did, despite not having paid much attention to anything in the papers, on the radio, or on television about what was to take place. I did not see anything to be worried about. After all, I had been taken on a "prize" trip to Washington, DC, seven years earlier with four white and eight Black kids. Everything felt normal to me except that we were billeted in separated hotels. We each had won the DC trip for prowess in selling new subscriptions to the *Charlotte News*. I still had a paper route but had "graduated" to a more lucrative *Charlotte Observer* early morning route. The paper route was how I afforded a car as a high school student.

Later that day, I learned that a large crowd had indeed gathered at the front entrance. But Gus and his father, who had filed a local lawsuit on behalf of Gus for admission citing *Brown v. Board of Education*, were able to stride past the parted crowd and up the ceremonial front steps to be greeted by Principal Ed Sanders. Sanders ushered the Robertses into the building and to his office where the three patiently worked out Gus's academic schedule for the fall semester. Across town at Harding High School, the situation was much different. By the end of the week, the one African American Harding student had withdrawn. I had reason to be proud of the way my school had accepted the inevitable. It was no big deal, I assured myself.

It was only recently that I found out Mr. Sanders had called the Central High football team to his office to tell them that they were all to be Gus Roberts's bodyguards. The football team members were to see to it that Gus saw no harm or experienced any disrespect. Sanders said any team members who showed disrespect, or caused harm to Gus, or failed in their duties in preventing any disrespect or harm to Gus Roberts from others, or who failed in their duties to keep the peace in general, would be kicked off the football team.

Genius moves on the part of Mr. Sanders. I and many of the football players had come to Central from Hawthorne Junior High where the football program had been eliminated four years earlier because of a large altercation that had broken out between opposing players and fans after a game.

Gus Roberts's enrollment, as the only Black student at Central High, proved to be a lonely existence for Gus. Gus and I shared no classes. I rarely saw him in the hallways, but I did see him in the cafeteria at times, almost always sitting alone. It would have taken no effort on my part to walk up to the table with my lunch tray and ask if I could share the table with him. No effort at all.

I did not avoid Gus because he was Black or for any other reason other than being preoccupied in my own little world of girls and cars. Complete and utter infatuation with a beautiful girl that I had been introduced to the first week of school and subsequently getting invited to her 16th birthday party put smoke in my eyes. That and my deep involvement with a small group of "car guys" who, like me, drove "cool" cars. My ride was lowered, had "lake pipes," a louvered hood, "flipper-style" hubcaps, a fresh paint job, and "hot rod" pin striping that I had applied myself having learned how to "stripe" watching Larry Watson from California stripe Don Garlits' "Swamp Rat IV" dragster at a drag strip near Chester, SC.

At lunch period, my car buddies and I would often be planning our next "rod hawking" excursions for the hours after school. Rod hawking was riding out in the rural areas around Charlotte looking for old cars that had potential as hot rods. While I was somewhat aware that Gus was lonely and felt out of place, my teenage self-centeredness prevented me from understanding what I should have done.

My indulgence in nonacademic pursuits also meant I barely graduated from high school. You had to have fifteen units to graduate. I only earned sixteen. Most students had twenty to twenty-two. They were focused on college. I was focused only on my girlfriend and modified cars. There were no clear plans for my future.

Post high school, every place I looked for work, I got the same reply: "We would like to hire you, son, but by the time we got you trained for the position, you'll be drafted." Hearing that comment repeatedly, I concluded I should enlist in the U.S. Air Force for the technical training possibilities, and I'd at least have a job for the next four years.

Prior to completing enlistment, one fall Saturday in November I was invited by guest-scheduler Arlene Clark, whose father was a local radio personality, to appear as a dancer, a shag dancer no less, on *Kilgo's Kanteen,* a local television station's version of Dick Clark's famous *American Bandstand.* During the broadcast, if you were not dancing, you were sitting around little tables like you were in a soda shop. During the show's broadcast, Mr. Kilgo came to my table and stuck his mike into my face and asked what I was going to do post high school. I was not expecting the question but gave my answer simply as "enlist in the Air Force."

Unknown to me at the time, Gus Roberts had enlisted in the Air Force directly after graduating from high school in June 1959. I enlisted on January 11, 1960. By mid-February 1960, I was awarded an exemption from what remained of boot camp and transferred to Chanute AFB in Illinois for tech school training to become a flight simulator operator.

At the base early one Sunday morning in April as I was approaching the dining hall entrance for breakfast, a skinny Black kid walked up to me and asked, "Do you know who I am?" I did not recognize Gus in uniform. He introduced himself saying, "I'm Gus Roberts; I graduated from Central High School with you, Class of 1959. I was home on leave between boot camp and tech school when I saw you on *Kilgo's Kanteen.* When you said you were going to enlist in the Air Force, I thought about trying to find your phone number to call you, to tell you don't do it, but I didn't because I thought you might not like advice from me." With that, Gus turned and walked away. I was dumbfounded, utterly speechless. That moment in time was the beginning of the realization that I had failed Gus Roberts as a member of the Central High School Class of 1959. I never saw Gus Roberts again.

Years later, I learned that after the Air Force, Gus returned to Charlotte. While Gus was always included in Class of '59 reunion invitations, he never attended any of the reunions. Perhaps for Gus, too many of the Central High Class of 1959 had also failed him.

Thinking about Gus occasionally, I thought about trying to locate him and call on him during one of my returns to Charlotte to visit family. My thinking was that I could personally encourage him to attend the next reunion. With a visit, I could assure him that his classmates would welcome his presence. I never called him.

In a minor way, Gus also failed me. He failed me by not getting in touch to tell me not to enlist. It's okay, I thought. I am glad Gus did fail me; otherwise, I may not have had the opportunity to marry Kathryn, my high school sweetheart, while in the Air Force; or enroll at Furman University while on active duty; or Clemson University; or graduate from North Carolina State University or Harvard University; or have had a wonderful experience in design practice; or fight fires with the Clemson University Fire Department; or design a fleet of fire apparatus; or drag race at the highest professional level; or most importantly, teach at Ball State University for three years and Clemson University for 33 years. Nor would I have had the opportunity to work with Clemson University to give birth to South Carolina's only Landscape Architecture degree.

Gus Roberts's little failure caused me no harm, but I often wonder if I and my classmates had failed Gus Roberts and made less than a sincere effort to befriend him at

Central High School. Would his life have played out any differently or would he at least have felt that he would be truly welcomed at a class reunion?

At one of the reunions, I learned Gus worked for the post office for a while and then operated a service station in east Charlotte. He died early. He was only in his early fifties.

Years later, there was a local news broadcast about Gus Roberts being the first Black student at Central High School. That news story about Gus showed where he is buried in an unmarked grave. Learning of the unmarked grave, I could have stepped up and paid for a suitable marker. I did not. Thankfully, someone stepped up and did their duty, for there is an appropriate marker there now.

But the marker's presence does not soothe my own regrets. I can only offer to you, Gus Roberts, my belated apologies for not stepping up. I am sorry for not befriending you when you may have needed a friend the most. I had the chance so many years ago. Forgive me, if you can, for failing you.

1965

Cecil Huey

I passed my college commencement date in a station wagon, along with four teammates and our coach, embarked on a weeks-long odyssey of track meets—first Houston, then Tempe, Bakersfield, and, finally, the NCAA championships in Berkeley. Our vehicle sported rear-facing seats that suited long legs and afforded a mesmerizing view of the continent drifting into the distance, a sight bound to stir philosophical musings. Things past were clear, but not things to come—same as life.

While in Bakersfield, we schemed with some guys from another team to travel to Yosemite for a day or so while our coaches amused themselves in San Francisco. The prospect of hanging out with a bunch from South Carolina disturbed one of their Black teammates, so the deal fell through. We were embarrassed upon sensing the problem and regretted not catching on soon enough to work things out. We went ahead on our own, though, unsupervised except for a later query concerning our filling up four times at the same Yosemite gas station. We made up something.

Nights were freezing in Yosemite so, by necessity, we wore our purple Clemson warm-up jackets around the park. Athletic wear had yet to become fashionable and ubiquitous, so we were noticed, and those jackets were our "in" with the California college students working there. They invited us to their evening revelry, and it was great. I envied them.

At Berkeley, we were housed on campus and there introduced to another pole of California college life and a campus where the Free Speech Movement was current, and Sproul Hall was a fresh memory. Little to envy here, we thought.

The anorexic limbs, listless bodies, bedraggled hair, grimy toddlers, and hollow stares from the people in the streets stunned our sheltered sensitivities and buttoned-down, penny loafer standards. These were not street people or hippie dropouts but the beginnings of a counterculture, and we couldn't see beyond them to the turbulent tide sweeping toward us all.

Like our Yosemite friends, I was slow waking to the Sixties.

Civil Rights Become Real

Victoria Ridgeway Gillis

In 1969-70, I was teaching seventh-grade science at a junior high in Athens, Georgia. I taught on a team of four teachers, each responsible for a different content area for the same group of approximately 150 students. It was the first year of forced busing in Athens. The year before had been the initial year of integration, allowing Black students to choose to go to all-white schools if they wished to do so. In 1969, the attendance lines had been redrawn, and integration was no longer a choice; it was enforced through busing.

I was in my second year of teaching that academic year and had been assigned all-Black classes. Next door, Claire Rutherford, the other seventh-grade science teacher, with over 25 years of experience, had all-white classes. In this way, the educational power structure ensured that the mandate to integrate met the requirement, if not the spirit, of the *Brown vs. Board of Education* decision handed down in 1954. This was by no means unique to Athens or to Hilsman Junior High.

The population of Hilsman Junior High came from two distinct and very different communities. Almost all the white students came from the subdivisions near the school that housed faculty who taught at the University of Georgia.

These students were relatively rich compared to the Black students who came from the poorest section of the housing projects in town. Many of my Black students arrived at school hungry, disheveled, and sleep deprived. White students arrived fed, groomed, and feeling entitled. These two populations were so different they might as well have come from different countries, and indeed they did in very real ways.

The first day of class I realized I could not understand a word my students spoke. I did not recognize my own name on their lips: "M-riway." For days, I worried about being unable to understand their speech, and then it dawned on me they quite possibly could not understand me. In addition, their cultural nuances were foreign to me—for example, their call and response to the roll call. After every name came a chorus of "Yo Mama," and "She do." Gradually, I began to understand the syntax of their Black Vernacular English and got accustomed to their ways of operating in the classroom. Ultimately, we were able to communicate with each other. I also came to know them personally as children who had been dealt a difficult hand in the card game of life. That year produced many stories I could tell, but the one I focus on here is illustrative of how white power structures present in small towns all over the South reacted to the *Brown vs. Board of Education* decision and the fallout from what I remember as the Summer of Death, the assassinations of Dr. Martin Luther King, Jr. and Robert Kennedy in 1968.

At the beginning of the 1969-70 school year, Black parents requested a holiday be added to the school calendar for Martin Luther King, Jr.'s birthday. He had been assassinated the year before, and the Black parents felt the school district should honor his sacrifice. To no one's surprise, the school board's answer was a resounding NO! As the school year began, an undercurrent of tension hummed every day as a guitar string would after being plucked.

In mid-January, Black students boycotted school for the week of King's birthday. It was eerie that week; my memory is one of quiet and, for me, a mostly empty classroom. Most of my students were absent the entire week. The Monday following the boycott, our principal called faculty in for an early morning faculty meeting before the buses arrived. I sat between Claire Rutherford and Margaret Dunston, two senior members of the faculty with over fifty years of teaching experience between them. The principal, Mr. Hevel, announced that any student returning to school without a written excuse from a parent or guardian should be sent to the gymnasium. We all looked at each other, stunned, as Margaret raised her hand and said "Mr. Hevel, are you certain about this? That might not be the wisest choice." He turned a beet-red face of fury to her and bellowed, "Are you questioning my authority in this matter?" Margaret replied, "No, sir," and then quietly to those of us sitting near her, "just your sanity." As a teacher still learning how to navigate the profession, I was horrified to hear Margaret and Claire verbally assassinate Mr. Hevel in hushed tones for the remainder of the meeting. When Mr. Hevel concluded the meeting, we all went to our classrooms to prepare for the day, dreading what might happen.

What happened was predictable to anyone with a brain. As soon as the Black students realized that friends without written excuses were being sent out of the classroom, they destroyed any existing excuses. As the minutes ticked by, more and more Black students were sent to the gymnasium. Once a critical mass of students had accumulated, they began to protest and then riot. They roamed all over the school, using chains, chairs, anything at hand that could be smashed or used as a weapon and destroyed all the artwork hung along the walls in the corridors. I could feel their rage, their feeling of helplessness and frustration. Because I had no students show up for first period class, I had gone to the library and was literally huddled with a few white students under a table in the library office while mayhem reigned in the halls. Once the school building had been thoroughly trashed, students set off to march to the district office, several miles away. This scene was repeated in other schools in the district. Protesting students were expelled for a week.

My students lost two weeks of instruction, and I lost my ignorance of another country, another America, foreign to me until that year. I taught in Athens for another two years, leaving in 1972. I've never forgotten that year, or the feeling of hopelessness that was so pervasive in my students or my feelings of inadequacy to address their needs.

Barely Working

Susan Hilligoss

Lots of people say their workplace is a zoo, but my first workplace *was* a zoo. Freshly graduated from high school, I got a summer job at the Indianapolis Zoo selling tickets and souvenirs. It was a great way to enter the world of work. While on the one hand there were timecards to punch, strict hours, and uniforms, on the other hand, most of the employees were teens, and as long as we cashed out the register correctly, we had little contact with adult staffers. And there were animals around us all the time, not to mention curious people attending on weekends, when the zoo was crowded. I had only lived in Indianapolis a year. For me the job gave freedom, coupled with the panorama and genial tolerance of life in the big city during summer.

The zoo was small, basically a children's zoo that had big aspirations since its opening two years before, in 1964. It occupied park land in an old, diverse neighborhood far from my suburban home on the northeast outskirts of town. The amenities were few but fun. There was a train for kids and parents to ride around the park. That summer a medical student was the engineer, when he wasn't at his other job driving an ambulance. The open-air souvenir stand was at the visitor entrance and exit, with one corner of the stand serving as a ticket booth. Two or sometimes three of us, all girls, were the cashiers and vendors. We wore white shirts and, over those, simple denim blue jumpers with the zoo's logo patch sewn on. (The logo featured a giraffe, but there was no giraffe! Visitors were disappointed.)

Our vantage point on the zoo itself was limited, but always interesting. First off, at the ticket window we saw everyone who came into the zoo. The tickets were inexpensive, and on sunny weekends the appeal of strolling through a park with interesting animals was strong. Families, teenagers, and young adults thronged through the turnstile. I had always lived where public spaces—schools, city pools, and parks—were integrated, at least nominally integrated, but it was at the zoo that I routinely saw interracial couples enjoying the sights.

The souvenir counter offered another vantage point, facing several attractions. To the left of the stand was the glass-walled penguin pool, where a half dozen or so Antarctic birds were always zipping through the water. Past the penguins was a small island, surrounded by a concrete moat, where a baby elephant was led several times a day to entertain visitors for an hour or so, depending on the heat of the muggy Indiana summer.

Everywhere, in front of our stand and throughout the zoo, peacocks roamed freely. Sometimes one would wander through the turnstiles, and we'd call the office to get some staff to shoo it back in. By staff I mean one or more assistant zookeepers—teenage guys and one girl—officially dressed like park rangers and wearing pith helmets. They led the elephant in and out of his exhibit area, helped the chief zookeeper in caring for animals, cleaned the penguin pool, and cleaned all parts of the zoo where animals went. They also hung out with us whenever things were slow, as on weekday mornings. Sometimes they'd bring an animal with them, like the tapir, which was named Watermelon because of the snazzy cream-colored horizontal stripes on his brown flanks. Watermelon walked on a leash just like a dog.

One day an assistant zookeeper came to our stand cradling a black bear cub in his arm. The cub, maybe a foot long, was hardly able to walk. It was not cute—quite ugly, in fact, like a tiny, grotesque boar with a pointed snout. Its head was about as long and wide as its curled-up body. The ears were little squiggles of flesh, the fur scraggly. Its eyes, which were up near the top of its head, were pale and strange. Not cuddly. The zookeeper put the cub on the souvenir counter. It tried to walk but its little bowlegs were mostly useless. I petted it. It turned its head and put its mouth on my hand, clamping the webbed skin between my thumb and forefinger. The cub squeezed. Hard. My hand was locked in its mouth. Uh-oh. Both the zookeeper and I worked to unhinge the cub's jaws, but the cub just squeezed harder. It was not sucking. This was a death grip. I wondered to myself if the med student was on site. Finally, I managed to work the skin—my skin! —out from the clenched gums. The cub's bite left impressions on my hand that lasted all day, but no blood. I'd seen a bunch of black bears and had once seen a young one almost outrun a tourist in the Smokies, but I never really understood their strength, even as little cubs. I was lucky.

Like a camp, the zoo had a party for its temp workers at the end of the summer. It was one evening after the zoo had closed for the day. A couple of the assistant zookeepers decided to swim with the penguins. They ditched their uniforms and jumped in. As I discovered that tiny bears are stronger than humans, these teenagers found out that penguins are way faster than humans, and they peck. Hard. We all left that job with some bruises but (mostly) fond memories.

If I ever appear on *Jeopardy!*, a condensed version of the baby bear story will be my human interest bit.

Strikers from the Medical University of South Carolina organize.

https://www.scencyclopedia.org/sce/images/14570/
Accessed September 22, 2025

Charleston, SC, 1969

Debra Broadwell Jackson

I returned to Charleston in January 1969 to complete my sophomore year of college. I was nineteen years old and enrolled at the Medical University of South Carolina (MUSC) in the College of Nursing. We were the only four-year undergraduate baccalaureate-seeking students on the campus. All our general education courses were taught by the Citadel (The Military College of South Carolina). Back in those dark days, exams were held after Christmas. There were no cell phones, no cable news in the dorm, and no free newspapers left in common areas. January was spent preparing for exams and planning for the next set of courses. Our "nursing student" uniforms were delivered, and we were measured to make sure the length was well below the knees—every other dress I owned had been shortened to well above the knees. We were preparing for our first clinical experiences and spent the latter part of January in a laboratory making beds, taking temperatures, measuring blood pressures, and practicing injections on each other.

If I say that I was a dedicated student, none of my peers would have been surprised. I studied. My roommate Carol studied. We had no distractions in our room: no television—no matter how small—no refrigerator, no phone; and no hot plate. We were first in line for every meal served and first for the shower each evening. One of us had a hair dryer (remember the hoods) on each evening to cut the noise in the dorm. I tell you this to let you know how surprised I was that there was trouble brewing in Charleston and at MUSC hospital among the staff. We were about to learn times were troubled.

Classmates from the Medical University of South Carolina, Class of 1971

Caducean, 1971, p.104
Courtesy of the Waring Historical Library
Medical University of South Carolina, Charleston, SC

Then, in March, we were surprised when we were called into our large auditorium classroom. I thought it was huge, and only now realize how small it was. It held maybe seventy seats, but it was tiered and looked very much like a traditional college classroom in movies. Mary Ann Kerr, our nursing faculty member, came in and told us about a strike of the workers at the hospital. Every African-American worker had walked out. Just the day before we heard that, for the first time, every bed at MUSC's teaching hospital was full. The walkout included not just the African-American nursing staff, but also Black nursing assistants, housekeeping, dietary, and laboratory staff.

I was stunned. Not afraid yet but stunned. How could you walk away from your patients? Our nursing theory and foundation courses had taught us about the commitment we were making to our patients as we became nurses. We had spent time in and out of the hospital for the last year and knew that most of the patients were Black and all the patients were poor people from the community. If you had money, you did not go to MUSC, you went to a nearby private hospital for care.

The next words from Ms. Kerr were that we were going to be in the hospital and providing basic care starting immediately, not in six weeks. Every nursing, medical, dental, and pharmacy student would be assigned immediate working responsibilities in the clinical environment in some place and in some capacity. As senior, junior, and sophomore students, we had some basic skills, but the first year medical and nursing students had yet to be in a clinical setting.

Some of my classmates were assigned to the nursery and had a wonderful time feeding infants. I was not so lucky. I was sent to a large medical floor and assigned to a group of patients. The charge nurse made assignments, and I was off to work. I recall one young woman whose name I do not remember, but I do remember her situation. I was sent to her room and told to help her eat. In an offhand way, I was informed that she was blind and deaf and had limited verbal interactions. I headed to her room and found her to be a young woman who was slightly shorter than me, and tiny. She needed a bath, her hair needed combing, and she needed to eat. I approached her and had no idea what to do. Should I touch her to let her know I was there? How should I communicate to her that it was time to eat? What the hell was I doing here, now, when I knew nothing? I left to find the nurse to ask her how to best approach her.

As I backed out of the room, an emergency code was called for the man across the hall. It seemed dozens of people responded and rushed in to help. I watched in horror as they struggled to revive him. The nurse turned as she rushed by me and said, "Your patient's food is getting cold!" I silently moved back into her room and touched her hand. She screamed. I jumped.

I wished I could say it was miraculous, that I'd connected to her. But I did help her eat, and she was cleaned and dressed before I left. I was afraid the entire day that I might hurt someone because I did not have the knowledge or skills to help them. I have blocked most of that day and the following days out of my memories. I did not like knowing that a person died across the hall, and I felt helpless to assist. I did not run away from the nursing profession. I did recognize what I needed to learn to be a better nurse and a better person.

Due to the walk-out, the Governor declared an emergency in Charleston, and we were under a dusk-to-dawn curfew for weeks or months. It seems like the entire semester shifted. The National Guard was housed in the nursing college building and were outside our classrooms. Picket lines formed and had to be crossed to get into the hospital. The guardsmen escorted us back and forth from our dorm to the hospital and to classes to ensure our safety. I knew that "outsiders" had been involved, but I doubt that I knew or even heard who had come to Charleston. I knew that many of the hospital staff had been threatened and warned that they had to strike or their families would be harmed. I do not know if that was true, but I tended to believe that it was.

What is amazing to me still is that my parents never called to check to make sure I was okay. I assume they did not think I was in danger. And I did not reach out to them either, which meant a collect call to our home number.

Communication was not what it is today. We continued classes and labs and working as we were assigned in the hospital. We prepared for our six weeks of required intensive summer clinical courses. The curfew was still in place as we started those summer classes. None of my classmates or myself ever considered not returning for the summer session. The strike continued, and we crossed picket lines to care for patients. The city was in disarray, but our world just moved as if things were normal. The Class of 1971 continued dwindling and by graduation fifty percent of our freshman class graduated in four years and one summer.

In 2008, I saw a television show about 1968 and the turbulent year it was, and I started thinking about where I was in 1968 and how I missed so much being in college. I wondered what I had also missed about the events in Charleston in 1969. No wonder I was shocked by the strike and marches that occurred. Those official reports and my memory were not in sync: while I knew what was happening around the hospital with the strike, I was unaware of the arrests, marches, and violence that was occurring just a short walk away.

MUSC records documenting the 1969 Hospital Workers Strike include the information that the strike began March 17, 1969, with the firing of twelve non-professional hospital workers. They had attempted to meet with then president, Dr. McCord, on March 16 to discuss the unionization of hospital workers, the establishment of a credit union, and an increase in wages. For 99 days, over 300 hospital workers walked out of their jobs and picketed the hospital.

The strike ended June 27, 1969, with the rehiring of the twelve discharged workers and an increase in the minimum wage. And the hospital started using timeclocks, a great boon for the staff and those of us who started to work part-time at the hospital to earn money. After that summer experience, we were termed "experienced" and hired at the same salary level as a Licensed Practical Nurse and given more responsibility. For me and others, this increase in salary and overtime pay, recorded by clocking in and out, was wonderful for staff and student workers. On a recent trip to Charleston, this marker was the only reminder of the strike I saw.

Historical Marker commemorating
the Hospital Strike of 1969

With permission of photographer, Debra B. Jackson, 2022

The Space Race

Apollo 11 Bootprint, July 20, 1969

Public domain, via Wikimedia Commons:
https://commons.wikimedia.org/wiki/File:Apollo_11_bootprint_-_GPN-2001-000014.
jpg

Accessed August 23, 2025

Sputnik, the Space Race, and Me

Victoria Ridgeway Gillis

In October 1957, the Union of Soviet Socialist Republics
(USSR) successfully launched and placed a satellite
named Sputnik into orbit. The news sent shock waves
through America. I can clearly remember standing in the
yard, looking up to try and spot the tiny starlike pinpoint of
light that moved steadily across the sky. That event brought
the United States up short and began what is often referred
to as the space race. The National Science Foundation
(NSF), charged with supporting science and engineering
in the U.S., geared up to increase their support for all
things science. Part of this initiative focused on improving
science teaching to produce more homegrown scientists and
engineers and to prepare more science teachers. The effects
of that program changed my life.

In 1964, I entered North Georgia College (NGC), a
small coeducational military college isolated in the North
Georgia mountains. I declared English as my major and
was unlucky enough to be selected for both honors English
and Chemistry that first quarter, although I had been
properly prepared. My high school English teacher focused
on writing, so my English placement test seemed easy.

The results put me in honors English. Furthermore, due to the NSF support of science education, I had had excellent science teachers in high school. My chemistry and physics teacher had replaced an incompetent science teacher just the year before I began high school. The replacement, Mr. Grant, had been an inspiring teacher. The results of my chemistry placement exam testified to that, as I qualified for honors chemistry. Science classes were the only ones I had ever studied for in high school, but I had not developed any systematic study habits. I spent that first fall at NGC playing bridge and drinking coffee in the canteen.

As I sat the English exam at the end of the quarter, I realized I had somehow missed something. The first question on the exam was: "Compose a sentence that contains a noun clause, an infinitive, and a gerund." What in the world was a noun clause? An infinitive? A gerund? My last grammar lessons had been in seventh grade and consisted of copying the grammar rules from the board. I got a "C" because I dotted every "i" with a circle, a small rebellion for a twelve-year-old. How on earth would I manage to pass this class? I thought back to English class discussions and couldn't remember whether any grammar had been mentioned. When my first-quarter grades were posted, I was in shock. I had never gotten grades that bad. The English professor had given me a "C," a gift if ever there was one. I immediately changed my major to biology and began to study in earnest.

My goal had always been to teach in high school. There was one hitch: NGC only had an elementary education major. Initially, I planned to complete two years at NGC then transfer to the University of Georgia, where I could major in secondary education. But as time passed, I came to love the small college atmosphere and searched for another route to my goal. I found the solution in a relatively rare program (at the time) called a Master of Arts in Teaching

(MAT), offered by fewer than a dozen colleges, all private and all expensive: Oberlin in Ohio (too cold), Harvard (are you kidding me?), Duke (again, are you kidding me?), Vanderbilt (too elite), and Emory, (also elite, expensive, but closer to home). Vanderbilt and Emory had NSF grants to produce secondary science teachers.

The Emory program was particularly innovative, with acceptance conditional on participants' performance during the first summer's methods course that primarily consisted of teaching thirty inner city Atlanta adolescents while being videotaped. Videotape technology was cutting edge media at the time. Each MAT participant had two days to teach a science concept, with teaching responsibilities rotated among us after an initial two-week demonstration by the Master Teacher in Residence. After each morning session, the professors "rolled the tape," and everyone critiqued the teaching. We acquired teaching expertise by learning from mistakes, our own and those of others. Or not. One of our number did not qualify for the MAT program and was advised to seek a "plain" master's in chemistry. The Emory MAT involved student-teaching through a paid internship, offering much needed financial help in addition to the tuition provided by the NSF grant. The Emory program was innovative in another way: it focused on preparing science teachers broadly. Because research indicated that physics and chemistry teachers were particularly scarce in the U.S., and those courses were often taught by unqualified teachers, my committee chose courses for my program that shored up my knowledge in physics and geology, two areas in which my background was weak.

The physics courses were taught by two well-meaning foreign graduate students who spoke a dozen languages, but English wasn't among them. I relied on what I already knew from my high school and college physics courses to muddle through. My geology class was fascinating because the theory of plate tectonics was in its infancy and was being widely panned by many geologists. My professor, however, was a devotee, and we focused on the evidence in support of the theory. The approach of this course reinforced what I learned in my philosophy of science course: that science was, first and foremost, a way of learning about the world. After majoring in biology, it was easy to assume that science was about memorizing "facts." But these two courses, along with discussions among my colleagues in science education, helped me develop a more accurate and broader view of science, influencing my approach to teaching. I earned my MAT from Emory, which meant I qualified to teach any high school science course. But I planned to teach biology.

I began my career at a junior high in Athens, Georgia, teaching life science. In my first year, I had students whose parents taught at the University of Georgia. One afternoon after school, one of those parents approached me and asked me to join his cohort of science teachers who were earning their master's degrees courtesy of his NSF grant. I declined, telling him I already had a master's degree. He was apparently desperate for participants, because he immediately said, "No matter, we can enroll you as a nondegree student, and you can work on your doctorate." I jumped at the chance. Taking science courses in the summers and being paid to do so was a dream come true. Books, tuition, and a stipend were covered by the NSF grant, and I got to do what I loved: learn more science. Mostly. One summer I did have to spend an inordinate amount of time in a stifling hot barn counting "bee wags" in an entomology course, collecting data for the professor. I managed to complete thirty hours of coursework toward a PhD in science education, which twenty years later actually still counted, precisely because I had completed them as a nondegree student. When I entered the PhD program in reading education at the University of Georgia in 1989, I focused my research on comprehension of scientific text and used those long-ago hours in my program of studies.

Had it not been for NSF grants, my high school science teachers might have been less effective. I could never have afforded a graduate degree from Emory. My PhD program would have taken longer. Sputnik inspired America to overhaul science education, and I benefitted from that effort. No one could have predicted in 1957 that I would profit at so many points in my life from that small Soviet object in the sky, but I certainly did. I taught K-12 science for twenty years, mostly physics and physical science, before returning to graduate school for a PhD in reading education. Ironically, high school biology was the only course I never taught.

Reasonable Doubt?

Cecil Huey

We witnessed Neil Armstrong's "small step" flicker across the black and white screen of our tiny TV perched on the edge of a homemade dining room table, rabbit ears positioned for best reception. At the time, I was employed as an engineer in the Offshore Division of the Humble Oil and Refining Company, located in New Orleans.

I spent several days a month "in the Gulf," meaning somewhere offshore, tending to the details of one project or another. Depending on the circumstances, I would hop about from site to site via helicopter or workboat. Boats were best except during wintry weather when stuffy cabins, rough seas, and whiffs of ever-present diesel fumes could nudge me to the edge of nausea. I preferred them because the boatmen were an interesting lot; helicopters were too noisy for comfort, and, when any "Bigs" were about, they were hard to depend on. Besides, the helicopter pilots, variously unsuited for Vietnam service, seemed interested only in flying and their next cigarette.

Roughnecks and roustabouts came from everywhere, some commuting hundreds of miles each week for the well-paying, seven-on, seven-off work schedule. Cooks in the living quarters more often hailed from the bayou region and along with meals they served a steady stream of "local color" for lagniappe. Homemade ice cream was served at every meal except breakfast.

Offshore oilfield work in those days might, in simple terms, have been characterized as moving a lot of heavy stuff around in tight quarters. It was tough work that demanded resourceful teamwork, and the hazards were many—I observed a disturbing number of hands no longer displaying five whole fingers.

I was there in the Gulf a few days after the Apollo 11 success, sweating in a yellow life jacket and hard hat, along with a couple of others, while waiting for a boat. An "old hand," once a trotline fisherman who "runned 400 hooks" to tease a living from the Louisiana swamps, was one of them. Now, secure in his settled role as "senior grump," he announced to all in earshot that the "whole damn moon thing" was faked. "How the hell they think I think I'm watching them guys up on the moon on TV when I can't even pick up Baton Rouge from my house?"

It was plain to see…

The Moon Landing

Clementina E. Adams

In Colombia, through the media, we were aware of the technological advances in the space era in the U.S. It was then common knowledge that the first humans to land on the moon were Neil Armstrong and Buzz Aldrin, aboard the Apollo 11 mission, on July 20, 1969. Armstrong became the first person to step onto the lunar surface, famously proclaiming, "That's one small step for [a] man, one giant leap for mankind."

Through my father's interest and research on space travel, we knew that the Apollo 11 mission took approximately three days and three hours to reach the lunar surface. However, it took about two days, 22 hours, and 56 minutes to return to earth. Unfortunately, our father was not able to explain that time difference. We also found out that there were six additional landings on the moon with six Apollo missions between 1969 and 1972. The missions during and after Apollo 11 resulted in a total of twelve astronauts landing and walking on the lunar surface.

Regarding the first walk on the moon, in my city, Barranquilla, Colombia, we were aware of the accomplishments of NASA through the media. We were not expecting a successful landing, nor that any human being would be able to actually step onto the moon. We could not grasp the idea of any human being daring enough to explore such frontiers. However, in 1969, there was an event that was etched in my memory forever. It was on July 20, 1969, during our Independence Day celebration in Colombia, a group of my friends and I went dancing at a disco club. That type of dance club offered food, drinks, music, and large TV screens. As always, we were having a fun time dancing and chatting. However, close to 11 PM, the music stopped suddenly, and everyone became silent. We all looked at the screens to see Neil Armstrong, the astronaut from the U.S. as he made history by being the first man to walk on the moon. There were cheers, clapping, and joy! Mankind had conquered space; what a marvelous concept and goal, now made a reality!

Neil Armstrong was 38 years old when he landed and walked on the moon on July 20, 1969. He was the commander of the Apollo 11 mission. I watched when they planted the U.S. flag on the moon, and more were planted during later landings. I imagine by now they might be totally destroyed and others partially deteriorated. It seems that flags planted on Apollo 12, 14, 15, 16, and 17 are still visible, based on Lunar Reconnaissance Orbiters. Overall, after Neil Armstrong's first step, eleven additional astronauts walked on the moon's surface.

Unfortunately, subsequent travel to the moon has not happened as expected. There have not been more missions, due to budgetary constraints, political shifts in NASA's priorities, and the inherent challenges of landing on and operating on the moon's surface. The focus turned to space shuttles, the International Space Station, and other goals.

I found it interesting as I learned that other countries had also gone to the moon after the Soviet Union's and the USA's visits to the moon. The following nations and organizations (in chronological order) have made similar visits, but without landing astronauts: Japan, the European

Space Agency, China, India, Luxembourg, Israel, Italy, South Korea, the United Arab Emirates, Russia, Pakistan, and Canada.

I believe that among all the decades I have lived, the sixties were my most significant and thought-provoking time. It covered a period of growth and discovery as a child, as a K-12 student, a college student, and a university student; also, periods of becoming a teacher, of postgraduate studies, and of social unrest, protests, whistleblowing, and social changes. It was also, for me, a time of profound personal and professional growth. What a time of excitement, joy, and expectations. I frequently wonder which planet will be next to receive pioneer astronauts and, in time, which planet will provide human beings with a new land to inhabit.

Aunt Peggy's Moon Flag

Don Collins

O n July 16, 1969, American astronauts Michael Collins, Buzz Aldrin, and Neil Armstrong blasted off from their launch pad at Cape Canaveral, Florida, atop a Saturn rocket to attempt mankind's first landing on the surface of the Earth's moon. The launch was the major milestone in what was the fulfillment of President John F. Kennedy's pledge, made early in his presidency, to put American astronauts on the moon before the end of the decade.

Just a couple of weeks earlier, I had been awarded my graduate degree from Harvard University. For the first time in seven years, I had no thoughts of academics on my mind, save my upcoming new position as an Assistant Professor at Ball State University in Muncie, Indiana. The new mind-freedom I was experiencing allowed me to focus almost entirely on the moon mission as it unfolded on my 12-inch black and white, rabbit-eared television.

Having packed much of our belongings and knocked down our furniture for shipment, my wife and I sat on the floor glued to the tube waiting for the next NASA news update. As the mission approached the moon, coverage was almost nonstop. From our thirteenth-floor apartment, I like to say we were closer to the moon landing than any of our friends or relatives.

On July 20, Armstrong landed the Lunar Module on the moon's surface while Collins remained in orbit around the moon tending to their return-to-Earth vehicle. It seemed like hours before they opened the hatch to exit their space craft. Armstrong was first to step off the Lunar Lander onto the moon's surface uttering his famous words, "One small step for man, one giant leap for mankind." My emotions were frayed. I was in awe at the achievement of the NASA program and the bravery of the three men on the mission, especially Armstrong and Aldrin, but at the same time I was suffering from a terrible sense of dread that something could go wrong at any point in the rest of the mission.

My foreboding did not keep me from watching as the two on the surface frolicked like two kids in a mud puddle as they experienced the weaker moon gravity. Thankfully, NASA engineers had sewn a patch to their spacesuit's wrist cuff with a to-do list to keep them focused on things to accomplish on the surface of the moon. One objective was to plant an American flag, to leave behind, as proof that American astronauts had been on the surface of the moon. As an ex-military man, I saluted their audacity when they planted that flag, a flag that would come to have a special meaning to me and members of my mother's large family.

My mother was one of eleven children. With that many children, there was bound to be at least one black sheep in the lot. Number six, right in the middle, was Olin. Olin was a rebellious child from the beginning, starting with adopting the nickname Pete in place of his given name Olin. In school he was often truant. As a high schooler, he often climbed out of his second-floor bedroom window during the night to take his dad's car for joyrides with his friends, long before he could drive legally. He, much like me, had to experience military discipline to gain a little bit of direction in his life. On discharge from active duty, that direction took him way across the city where he took up with a new flame named Peggy. Before his parents and siblings even got to know much about her, they eloped to South Carolina and were married. No church wedding, nor anything else that went with a public wedding, for Pete and Peggy.

True to form, they took up residence on Peggy's side of the city. Nevertheless, they did occasionally attend a family social function like Thanksgiving, Christmas, or Easter. When Pete and Peggy attended, she always, in my memory of her, had a wry smile on her face that said, "I have a little secret, I know something that you don't know." Neither seemed at ease at family events. Aunt Peggy didn't talk much, but when she did, you took notice.

The three American astronauts returned to Earth on July 24, 1969. The next summer, my wife and I, along with our young son, returned to our hometown for the first time since graduate school for a family event. At some point during the gathering, the moon landing of the previous summer came up in the conversation banter. I don't remember who brought the moon landing up. It may have been me, for Aunt Peggy looked at me with the same wry smile she always had and said, "I made the flag that was planted on the moon. I even embroidered my name on the inside of the hemmed tube at the top of the flag, the tube used to slide the flag over the horizontal bar attached to the flagpole."

Today, some people believe the moon landing never took place. They claim the whole thing was staged on a movie set somewhere. They point to the "waving" flag as proof that an atmosphere was present, and the wind was blowing. I only know what I saw on the television coverage. When I look at the pictures of the moon flag, I see a flag made of a stiff fabric. Fabric so stiff it acquired creases in transit to the moon's surface.

`I cannot verify that the landing took place. Nor can I verify Aunt Peggy's story about making the very flag planted by Armstrong and Aldrin on the moon or her incredible declaration about embroidering her name on the inside of the flag's top hem. But I can verify that she worked for a flag company as a seamstress, a company owned by Pete's oldest brother. Because of that connection, I have no reason to really doubt Peggy's declaration. I guess we will just have to have another moon mission for an investigation to corroborate both NASA's accomplishment and Aunt Peggy's claim to fame.

Buzz Aldrin salutes the U.S. flag on the moon.

The Whole World Was Watching

Marty Duckenfield

The Sixties were a time of renewal after the postwar years, culminating in the end of Dwight Eisenhower's presidency and John F. Kennedy's election. The new president's inaugural address signaled a passing of the torch to a new generation, of men and women who had fought in the war and were seeing the world through changed eyes. They had become realistic about addressing both the flaws of America as well as its idealism for greater aspirations. The most popular of these was putting an American on the moon. The excitement Kennedy's challenge generated during the sixties was shared by all.

Throughout those years, I followed the astronauts with great interest. When the decade was nearing its conclusion and it appeared the goal of the first moonwalk was about to be reached, I found myself in an unexpected location.

My husband Chris and I were on board the new Cunard vessel, the QE2, in the middle of the Atlantic Ocean, all our worldly possessions in two trunks in the hold of the ship as we immigrated to England for the next adventure in our lives. Our timing, however, coincided with another voyage that was much more significant—at least to the world—

and that was the voyage of Apollo 11, with its passengers
of Neil Armstrong, Buzz Aldrin, and Michael Collins.
The ship's daily news briefing kept us informed about
their progress.

The date was July 20, 1969, and the goal to land on
the moon by the end of the decade was about to reach
fruition. Without the reporting of Walter Cronkite keeping
us informed, we had gone to the deck that evening based on
the ship's morning update. We stood, staring into the night
sky, where we saw a partial moon.

"Don't you feel like we should be able to see them up
there?" I asked Chris, pointing to the moon. "The night is
so clear!"

At that moment, surrounded by a vast ocean with
nothing between us and the moon, I felt a direct connection
to what was unbelievably occurring so far away. Chris
smiled in answer to my question. I knew that we couldn't
see the event happening; nevertheless, we were still in awe
of what we imagined was taking place, so far away on that
partial moon.

After we landed in Southampton, we turned our thoughts
and our journey to the trip to Lancashire, where Chris
would begin his job search. En route north, we made a brief
diversion, going through Wales and stopping by Caernarfon
Castle, where Prince Charles had only recently been
invested as Prince of Wales by his mother, the Queen.

While enjoying an ice cream cone near the castle, we
suddenly heard familiar voices. It was Chris's aunt and
uncle and their two children, Chris's young cousins Gillian
and Martin jumping up and down with excitement—
after all it was quite unexpected. But the reality was,
though thrilled to see us, they were even more excited to
talk about the moon landing. Nine-year-old Gillian had
an encyclopedic knowledge about the astronauts, their
activities on the moon, and Michael Collins circling the

moon waiting to pick up Armstrong and Aldrin. By that time, she had already seen on TV that the astronauts had safely landed back on earth, which she recounted in great detail. Thus, we got our first full news report—once again, not from Walter Cronkite but from a very reliable source, a nine-year old English school girl on a holiday visit to Caernarfon.

It wasn't just Gillian, either; the entire country of England had been transfixed by the event. Since then, I have learned that the entire world was glued to their TV sets during those tense and exciting days while we were at sea. We eventually got caught up, watching the films on TV, but I always regretted not having Walter Cronkite tell me about the event in real time. Cronkite's broadcasting the news gave it an official American stamp of approval.

Later, in April 1970, having settled on the Wirral Peninsula just across the Mersey from Liverpool, I was in another unexpected location during a dramatic space event. Once again, I was somewhat cut off, not only from Walter Cronkite but also from seeing any of the events the entire rest of the world got to see on their TVs. At that exact moment, I was in the expectant mums' ward of Clatterbridge Maternity Hospital, there for a two-weeks-long resting stay prior to my twin sons being born, and Apollo 13—of "Houston-we-have-a-problem" fame—created a nerve-wracking distraction for the eight of us in the ward.

Aside from the Beatles' split-up just a week before, this was the most serious world event to reach our ears, and we all were anxious about the safe return of the astronauts. The good news arrived, this time from another alternative to Walter Cronkite—one of our midwife nurses— after several very tense days. Apollo 13 astronauts were safely back on earth, a happy ending for the astronauts.

The excitement and thrill of space travel captured the imagination of the world, which was indeed watching, even in this tiny corner of England. The postwar generation expanded all of our aspirations for a brighter future, and the space program led the way.

Vietnam

Private First-Class Russell R. Widdifield in Vietnam, 1969

Public domain, via Wikimedia Commons:
https://commons.wikimedia.org/w/index.php?search=Private+First+Class+Russell+R.+Widdifield+in+Vietnam%2C+1969&title=Special%3AMediaSearch&type=image

Accessed August 23,2025

Union, Student, and Worker Protests

Clementina E. Adams

The sixties, an era of unrest around the world, saw students all over Europe, the United States, and Latin America becoming aware that they could and must openly express their discontent with the established political systems and especially with often unnecessary wars and their catastrophic consequences. My fellow students and I became more active in demanding positive changes in both government and universities. In my college, the University of Atlantico, in Barranquilla, Colombia, protests were usually carefully organized, and both justifications and rationale were discussed and analyzed at student meetings. Students then would vote either way, and the majority of votes would prevail. Workers' strikes, too, have long been a strategy of "the people" to demand needed changes, which students supported in solidarity. Student speakers stated their reasons for a strike and the pros and cons of it.

Once a strike was declared, most students would take to the streets marching, holding posters, and chanting in a chorus to proclaim the problems and workable solutions. When we were overwhelmed by excessive police force, we would run to evade apprehension. Some students were inevitably captured and taken to jail until their parents would come rescue them. In my house, only a couple of my brothers were taken into custody for marching in protests. My parents talked to the police and managed to get them freed. When I marched, I always looked for areas with bushes where I knew I could hide out in case of police chases.

Seniors and upper-class students were usually the leaders and a powerful voice at our college. Among the leaders, there was one called Vallejo, whom I considered to be a true leader. He had charisma and an easy but firm communication ability. I saw his effectiveness on one occasion when a majority of students voted not to go on strike. Then Vallejo, who had been absent at the time of the voting, appeared and explained the situation in such a straightforward way that we agreed to take a second vote, and the result was a total reversal of the first vote. It was the first time that I had witnessed the effects that a charismatic leader can have on others. I soon became aware that these kinds of protests and marches were also happening in North America, Europe, and many other countries.

Several years later, while I was working in Bogotá, as the Coordinator of the Multinational Center for Instructional Technology, I met Vallejo again. He was then Dr. Vallejo and director of one of the branches of the national educational system of Colombia. Through the ironies of life, yesterday's "rebel" had become the "established leader" of today. His knowledge and experience of the past served us greatly in the improvement of the educational system in Colombia.

One of the international situations that got students' attention at my university was the war in Vietnam, which we were informed was caused by an internal conflict in the country, with North Vietnam advocating for a communist regime and South Vietnam supporting a democratic system. It was, in essence, an ideological conflict between communism and democracy, a side effect of the Cold War, with the United States trying to prevent the spread of communism in the world. The United States' intervention in Vietnam would lead to a prolonged and devastating war.

In Colombia, the general opinion was that the U.S. should not have interfered in Vietnam's civil war. As in the U.S., college students in Colombia and even labor unions organized protests against intervention in Vietnam, calling for the U.S. to withdraw. The students' reactions were energized by the facts that they saw on TV and read in newspapers about how many young people in the U.S. were also against that war.

There were good reasons for Colombians to oppose the Vietnam War; one of them was the fact that this was the first "televised war." People across the world saw heartbreaking images on television, which led to a growing sense of disillusionment. Many questioned whether the war was necessary and how effective it had been. Another factor in the opposition was the high number of casualties, with 58,279 American military personnel eventually killed, in addition to an estimated three million Vietnamese military and civilians. That did not include the considerable number of wounded and disabled veterans on both sides. The bodies of American service men and some women were returned in coffins draped with the U.S. flag, one of the constantly repeating and poignant images of the war. Other cruelties of the war were the use of napalm and Agent Orange by the U.S. military, with side effects including widespread environmental damage as well as long-term health problems for the ones fighting as well as those living within the war zones as well as the My Lai massacre.

While there's no record of Colombian soldiers participating in the Vietnam War, according to the United Nations Command (UNC) and the U.S. Department of

Defense, Colombian soldiers had previously fought in support of the U.S. For example, during World War II, more than 15,000 Colombians served in the armed forces overseas; of those, approximately 450 service men were reported to have been killed.

During the Korean war, the UNC reports that Colombia sent the "Colombian Battalion" to support the U.S. war efforts in Korea. Colombia sent four to five battalions, with approximately 4,314 to 5,100 infantry soldiers, with 300 sailors on frigates who served in Korea between 1951 and 1954.

During the Vietnam war, U.S. troops fought in Cambodia, Laos, and from bases in South Korea, Thailand, Mainland Japan, Guam, and on Okinawa, where my husband was stationed for eighteen months, while in the U.S. Air Force.

According to the Military History Institute of Vietnam (2002), the Vietnam War led to a shift in American military strategy. The war's unpopularity, loss of lives, and excessive costs of the involvement in that conflict prompted a rethinking of American military intervention abroad, a reevaluation that followed a period of intense debate and political pressure after the signing of the Paris Peace Accords in January 1973. However, a number of U.S. military advisors remained in South Vietnam to protect U.S. facilities and personnel. The War officially ended on April 30, 1975, when North Vietnamese forces overran Saigon, the capital of South Vietnam. Over the course of the Vietnam Era (1961-1975), approximately 9 million U.S. military personnel served on active duty.

In Colombia, we were saddened by the tragic loss of lives and the life-changing wounds of war, both physical and psychological. When I came to the U.S. in 1973, I observed Americans' dissatisfaction with the war: the antiwar marches, the sit-ins, and ongoing discourses reported by national and international media that showed the true devastation. Included in my memoir here is a photo of Florida State University students marching to put an end to the war; it was taken in Tallahassee, in the early 1970's. Some of my classmates were Vietnam veterans who had returned to study at FSU, some missing limbs, some in wheelchairs and showing signs of distress and a sadness that made them look older than their years.

The Vietnam War was one of those situations where neutrality on the part of the U.S. might have worked better than intervening in the civil conflicts within another country. Unfortunately, since the Vietnam war, America has participated in the Kosovo War in 1999, the Gulf wars, and in Afghanistan. The current fear of getting involved in another war against Iran looms over us as I write this. Yet we can and should strive for a better future, united, fair, and peaceful.

FSU students marching for anti-war protest in Tallahassee, Florida, 1970.

State Archives of Florida, Florida Memory. <https://www.floridamemory.com/items/show/25387>

Accessed October 10, 2025

Growing Through the Sixties

Dolores (Dee) Stegelin

A time of personal and national tragedy. For many people, the Vietnam War came at a time in their lives that had a very disruptive impact. For me, the years just prior to the Vietnam War were filled with trauma, and the Vietnam War became the last of a trifecta of major experiences in my life.

In the spring of my junior year in high school, my father, a robust and healthy dairy farmer, became very ill and was diagnosed with terminal cancer. We learned of this in June 1964, and after several months of intense radiation and other medical interventions, he died in January of 1965, in the middle of my senior year of high school. I was the oldest daughter and very close to my father, and his death was a traumatic experience for me, and my entire family; my mother was left to raise four children between eleven and nineteen years of age.

With lots of support from my high school friends, teachers and administrators, I completed my high school years and graduated in the spring of 1965. In the fall of 1965, I started college at Kansas State University, a land grant university in Kansas just 45 miles from our farm near Abilene. Looking back, it was not a long distance in miles, especially by today's standards, but then it seemed like a million miles away from my family and home, and the farm I grew up on. Beginning college in the fall of 1965 was a mixture of excitement, anticipation, and lots of guilt for leaving my mother and siblings on the farm for the first time since my father's recent death.

It took time and maturity, but I came to understand that although the Sixties brought great sadness and loss—the loss of President Kennedy, my own father, MLK, and RFK—the latter part of the Sixties brought me personal growth and great joy. Kansas State University was a wonderful place for a first-generation farm kid to go to college. The land grant mission was very visible, with a student-focused learning environment and curriculum, supportive faculty members who went to great lengths to know their students, and innovative financing options for students just like me, who were excited to go to college yet had few resources to meet that goal.

Looking back, I realize that I found myself at KSU; it was a perfect match for a student with my profile and needs. I loved every course I took, and I switched majors twice before settling on child development, which I had great confidence in choosing.

Extracurricular activities and scholastic honorary groups were a big part of my life. Collegiate 4-H and the Wesley Student Foundation kept me grounded as I grew to independence and forged my future. I met my future husband, Forrest, at KSU, graduated *magna cum laude* in 1969, and completed a master's degree on full scholarship in 1970—a very significant year: graduation, marriage, and becoming an Air Force wife. I survived the Sixties and learned how to thrive, even with great pain and loss, and perhaps because of it. The year 1970 was not only the transition into a new decade, but it also marked the end of the turbulent Sixties and, for us, the beginning of our dealing with the Vietnam War.

I was about to discover that the 1970s were going to be very eventful, too: Vietnam trauma, rejoining the civilian community, and bringing two babies into the world. Yes, the early Seventies would be significant and very eventful and still tied to the Sixties which will go down in my personal history as the most impactful decade of my life.

The Vietnam War: my story. By 1970, I had earned two degrees to prepare me for my professional goals, met my college sweetheart, Forrest, and we had committed ourselves to our personal journey. We married in February 1970 and immediately embraced the military commitment that came with the Vietnam Era. My husband's number in the draft lottery was precariously high, so he had decided to fulfill his military role through the Air Force ROTC at Kansas State. With that commitment came a five-year military obligation, beginning with Officer Training in California to be a B-52 Navigator. Being farm kids from Kansas made our adjustment to military life even more challenging—everything was new to us! But that didn't matter: the military commitment had to be fulfilled before we could move forward with our lives.

Leaving the plains of Kansas as college graduates to become an Air Force officer and wife in Sacramento, California, was an exciting move and experience for us. We traveled on the weekends, camped in the sequoias of Northern California, and embraced the new California lifestyle. California was also a source of social unrest— Charles Manson and Angela Davis, for example—and such things were a shock to our midwestern world view. But California was also fun and exhilarating. Forrest received navigator training for nearly two years in Sacramento, and then we were assigned to Barksdale AFB in Bossier City, Louisiana, a sister city to Shreveport. We arrived in Louisiana in late 1971. At that same time, Nixon decided to utilize B-52 bombers to end the Vietnam War through massive and intensive bombing. Thus, my husband's entire class of newly trained navigators were all assigned to the same make and model of airplane: the B-52.

I had an ominous feeling when he graduated in Sacramento and got his assignment to B-52s rather than less dangerous carrier planes. I was uneasy, and the war's resistance was growing. Still newlyweds, we moved from sunny, exciting California to the heart of the Deep South. With the president's new focus on ending the war soon by using B-52s, I suspected that uncertain adventures awaited us.

In the spring of 1972, we moved to a rental house near the base in Bossier City, where we had no family support and very few friends. The moment we relocated, Forrest's B-52 crew was deployed with only three-days' notice to a military base in Guam for one year. The B-52s were to help end the Vietnam War through large-scale bombing of critical infrastructures in Vietnam, especially around Hanoi. These rapid, life-altering changes were shocking to a newlywed couple who had only just celebrated their second wedding anniversary.

Forrest's B-52 crew (and nearly the entire Barksdale AFB personnel) were relocated to Guam in April 1972. Eight months later, in December, Forrest's crew was assigned to the inaugural flights of the Christmas Raids, directly over Hanoi in an effort to free the POWs. On December 22, in the middle of the night, Forrest's B-52 was shot down, and the crew members were rescued by U.S. military, alive but injured. Two days later, on Christmas Eve, Forrest's crew returned home to the base in Bossier City, Louisiana. Every crew member had been injured in the low-altitude bailout after being hit by a surface-to-air-missile. We were stunned at the turn of events in such a short period of time, but we felt very grateful that all had survived this event when so many of our friends were either captured or killed in their missions. We also felt fortunate as the other crew members experienced more serious injuries; the pilot spent six months in Walter Reed Medical Center with a fractured back.

After a thorough medical evaluation, Forrest was told that he could not fly again for the Air Force due to the injuries he had sustained in the B-52 crash. Due to his back injury, Forrest would not be able to sustain such an event again. In some ways, this news was a relief. On the other hand, we knew with more limited options as an officer, our military adventures were likely over since he was permanently grounded from flying. Alas, we would fulfil our military commitment and then move on. Our son, Stephen, was born in the fall of 1973 in the Barksdale AFB military hospital, and our military commitment was fulfilled by late 1974 with an early-out option. We had survived the Vietnam War, and we had grown a great deal individually and as a couple.

Maturity gained: post-Vietnam. As I look back on this time in my life, the impact of the Vietnam War really began while Forrest and I were in college in the Sixties with his decision to embrace the ROTC route as his military commitment. The tumultuous societal events of the Sixties had somehow merged into the traumatic events of the early Seventies, creating a long decade of personal, national, and global events that shaped our lives forever.

After our experience with the Vietnam War, Forrest and I were ready to take on civilian life after a nearly five-year, intense military experience. The post-Vietnam 1970s led to doctoral degrees for both of us, the birth of our daughter, and a journey into higher education. The events of our lives in the Seventies were the result of the significant decisions and experiences of the Sixties: the assassination of so many vibrant people, the turmoil of the Vietnam War, and the post-war America that followed. It is not possible to separate the events of the Sixties from the events of the 70s. They are intertwined, both personally and professionally. We came of age in the Sixties and then we re-found ourselves again in the Seventies. Thank goodness.

Revisiting the Vietnam War in 2025. On a recent 2025 visit to Barksdale AFB in Bossier City, LA, after fifty years away, I had the opportunity to see the new Vietnam War Monument at the Air Museum on the AFB. After all these years, it was an existential moment to see my husband's name on this monument, honoring the B-52 crews who were lost or rescued in the Christmas Raids of December 1972. The Linebacker II Initiative was put in place by Nixon and the Pentagon to end the war through strategic bombing by B-52's of sites in Hanoi. Engraved on this monument are the names of all crew members whose B-52s were shot down by SAMs (surface to air missiles) during the Raids. Of the lost crews, only two crews were completely rescued, and Forrest's crew was one. Unlike his lost comrades, Forrest has 50-plus years of life to look back on and appreciate. Seeing this monument fifty years after the 1972 fateful event was indeed a sobering moment.

On this return trip to the AFB, we also visited a very special woman, Wilma, who was the school secretary at the high school where I was teaching science at the time of the Raids of 1972. Now in an assisted living center in Bossier City, LA, Wilma is 85 years old and as engaging as ever. Her husband was an NCO and a mechanic on the B-52s sent to Guam, along with my husband and the B-52 flight crews. During the 1972 Raids, she noticed that I, a new military wife alone on a new AFB, was really struggling. Wilma gently took me under her wing and probably saved my life, as I became very ill during this time, much of it from stress. She came to my house to visit me daily when I was ill, fixed me meals, but mostly she encouraged and supported me throughout the ordeal. Without Wilma, I'm not sure I would have made it through these tough eight months. In retrospect, this was an existential time in our young lives. We went through a lot individually and as a couple. Now, fifty years later, I am forever grateful for the outcome of this experience, for without Forrest's rescue, I would not have had a husband or my future children. And now we can look back over 50-plus years, a gift that many of these brave B-52 officers never had the chance to do.

Linebacker I monument

On the Catawba River: A Memoir

Stephen H. Wainscott

In *The Things They Carried,* Tim O'Brien offers a collection of stories about his experiences as a soldier in Vietnam. The genre of the book is metafiction, meaning that he mixes real place names, experiences, and persons (including himself) with fictional characters and stories that blur the distinction between reality and make-believe.

In the chapter "On the Rainy River," O'Brien tells of graduating from college and losing his student draft deferment. One day he sets out from his parents' suburban home in Minnesota to think about his options. Near the U.S. border with Canada, he encounters an elderly farmer who takes him in and offers to pay him for work on the farm. During O'Brien's stay, he never talks about Vietnam and his internal struggle, yet the old man knows what he is going through.

One day the farmer takes O'Brien fishing on the Rainy River. The old man quietly works his lure around the water as O'Brien sits in the back of the boat not speaking a word, just staring at the riverbank. As the old man steers the boat close to the shore, O'Brien realizes that with just one leap he could escape to Canada and be relieved of his internal turmoil ("I gripped the edge of the boat, leaned forward and thought now!"). But he cannot bring himself to do it.

The next day as he prepares to leave—for home and eventually to Vietnam—he sees an envelope under his pillow that contains four fifty-dollar bills along with a note: "emergency fund." Yes, the old man knew.

On the drive back home, O'Brien is ashamed that at the moment when he could have shown the courage of his convictions, he failed: "I was a coward. I went to war."

My Rainy River. The Catawba River runs north-south a few miles west of Charlotte, NC, my hometown. Unlike the Rainy River, it is muddy and stressed by pollution. And crossing it doesn't take you to Canada to escape from the draft. Yet for me it provides a background for a story of personal turmoil similar to O'Brien's.

During my early college years, my views concerning the war in Vietnam were much like O'Brien's: mixed, soft, fluid. On the one hand, I could understand the view of many that it was a noble cause to stem the tide of communism. On the other hand, I could see it as an unnecessary and ill-advised intrusion into another country's civil war, and an adventure that was unlikely to end well. But when Barry Goldwater in his 1964 campaign talked recklessly about using nuclear weapons in Vietnam, my views started to congeal. Upon entering graduate school in 1967 I found that most of my fellow students' views were distinctly antiwar. And they made sense to me. Thus, I ended up a fan of Eugene McCarthy, and I rejoiced when LBJ announced that he would not seek re-election in 1968.

Midway into my second year in graduate school, the Selective Service System ended 2-S draft deferments for graduate students. Early in January 1969 I received a letter from my draft board in Charlotte informing me that my status had been changed to 1-A: draft bait. Soon thereafter

I started receiving many letters and phone calls from my father who repeatedly asked me what I planned to do about my "military obligation." That question always drew an angry reaction from me because (1) my father never served in the military, and (2) my increasingly antiwar views had led me to reject the notion that I had a "military obligation."

A few weeks later, Dad called again. "I just got off the phone with your draft board," he said, "and your name is coming up soon, possibly as early as next month. You'd better come home and do something about this, or your ass is going to be grass, and Uncle Sam is the lawnmower." Yes, he really said that.

At this point, allow me to digress into a few ruminations about, well, about life. During this anxious time, I learned that life is not a multiple-choice test but about real-life and often in-the-moment decision-making. Understanding that, I proceeded to take control of circumstances—to the extent that Uncle Sam allowed me to do so.

The first thing I did was to go to Charlotte and have a heart-to-heart with my parents. By this time my father, who in 1964 agreed with Goldwater that the U.S. should "bomb Vietnam back to the Stone Age," had become harshly critical of the war, saying that it was "immoral." I agreed with him, but for different reasons. Dad thought that the war was immoral because he didn't believe Johnson had the backbone to bring the war to a successful military conclusion. I argued that the war was immoral because the U.S. was taking sides in another country's civil war.

"Ok, son, I understand, but what are you going to do? Understand that I will support you no matter what you decide, but you must decide—and right soon." I needed to hear that. I proceeded by going through what I perceived to be my "options." Like O'Brien, I said that I would consider going to Canada. Or, I would claim to be a conscientious objector. Or, I would just say, "Hell no, I won't go" and do time as a draft dodger.

Enter reality, stage right. Could I *really* flee to Canada and risk never being able to come home again? Could I *really* try to convince my draft board that I was a pacifist, knowing that there was nothing in my background that would remotely indicate that? And, to be serious, could I *really* give Uncle Sam the finger and accept being sent to prison for draft evasion? Really means reality.

After accepting that being an expat wasn't in the cards, that pretending to be a Quaker was a non-starter, and that having a criminal record wasn't how I wanted to spend the rest of my life, I accepted the reality that Uncle Sam was going to be my lawnmower. The only decision I had was under what terms I, like O'Brien, would be a "coward."

From that point on, I accepted that military service was unavoidable. I determined that every decision I was to make would be based on a singular objective: minimizing my chances of going to Vietnam and having my ass shot off.

So, my first decision was that I would be a draft dodger, not by refusing military service altogether, but by enlisting. Much as the idea of volunteering to bear arms stuck in my craw, the cost-benefit notions rumbling around in my head suggested to me that doing nothing and waiting to be drafted would likely increase my chances of ending up in Vietnam and losing my derriere.

The second decision was how I would enlist and under what terms. Plan A was to get a slot in a local National Guard or Army Reserve unit. Do the standard eight weeks of basic training, followed by eight weeks of advanced training, then come home to play soldier one weekend a month for four years. Chances of going to Vietnam? About as much as being hit by lightning. So, I made the rounds to Guard and Reserve units in and around Charlotte, only to be told that there were no openings.

In fact, there were openings, just not for people like me. Getting a spot was easy if your family was wealthy or your daddy was influential in the community. Alas, the Wainscotts were neither.

With weekend warrior out of the picture, I embarked on Plan B: regular enlistment. In doing so, I immediately ruled out the Marine Corps, because I was hardly a gung-ho type who preferred crawling through jungles with a dagger between my teeth to driving around Charlotte on a Saturday night.

My first recruiting visit was to the Air Force, my rational calculus suggesting to me that, except for the long-range bombing of Hanoi and Vietcong supply trails, the Air Force seemed relatively safe and out of the way of ground combat. Similar assumptions were in the back of my mind when I met with a Navy recruiter. The only problem was that both the Air Force and the Navy required a four-year commitment.

That left the Army, the branch that shouldered most of the ground combat role in Vietnam. Given my overriding objective of returning from service with all body parts intact, what sense did that make? I learned that the Army required a three-year commitment, thus presenting a dilemma: four years of duty, but likely away from the heat of battle, versus three years of service, with a year of that quite possibly involving shooting and being shot at. The Army became more attractive when the recruiting sergeant informed me of an option: Officer Candidate School, a rigorous six-month training program that when completed resulted in being commissioned as a second lieutenant. The thought occurred to me that being an officer just might afford me a smidgen more control over my fate than if I were an NCO (non-commissioned officer, such as a corporal), especially a drafted one.

On June 24, my mother's birthday, I acted out my cowardice and entered the Army. Following basic combat training and advanced training in artillery fire direction control, I went to OCS at Fort Belvoir, Virginia, and was commissioned in Military Intelligence in May 1970. My initial orders read: "SEA NLT 571." Meaning Southeast Asia, no later than May 1971. Meaning Vietnam. When I saw this, my reaction was that I had outsmarted myself and that all my calculations intended to avoid coming home in a body bag had been for naught.

But wait! Final orders for Vietnam were never issued, and I ended up spending the rest of my Army time as an intelligence publications editor at Fort Bragg, North Carolina. Hardly cloak and dagger stuff, but the work was interesting and even fun. (I often joked that my greatest accomplishment as an intelligence officer was keeping the Vietcong from crossing the nearby Cape Fear River.)

Side story. One weekend my wife Sue and I were going to spend a weekend at my parents' house in Charlotte. Sue picked me up at my place of work, which meant that I didn't have time to change into my civvies. We stopped along the way to gas up. A station attendant saw me in my dress green uniform and asked me what that starburst on my uniform lapel was. I explained that it meant I was in military intelligence. After eyeing me suspiciously for a few seconds, he asked in perfect English, "Mister, is you a spy?"

At Bragg I joined the Officers' Club and was able to play golf twice a week for $12 a month. Our son was born at the post hospital. The delivery cost was $5.25 (we still have the receipt, just in case he ever says he doesn't owe us anything). I was able to get my teeth fixed at no cost. On Fridays my buddies and I would meet at the Officers' Club for happy hour and enjoy 25-cent martinis, after which we would eat steak dinners with wine for $3.50. Life at Fort Bragg was not half bad.

In December 1971, word came down from the Department of the Army that due to the winding down of U.S. involvement in Vietnam, there would soon be a reduction in force. On January 14, 1972, I received an "early out" and was honorably discharged with derriere intact. I also was awarded the Army Commendation Medal, presumably for stopping the communists from crossing the Cape Fear River.

Two brothers' experiences: yin and yang. In January 1970, when I was being beaten up on the physical training fields of Fort Belvoir, my younger brother John faced his own Catawba River moment. Having dropped out of college, he lost his student deferment and in short order received his induction notice. John notified the draft board that he did not intend to show up for his induction and requested SSS Form #150 for purposes of claiming conscientious objector status. On the form he described his religious beliefs: "I believe that to harm or destroy any human being is to endanger any hope for peace; to me, it is morally unpardonable. Therefore, I cannot and will not participate in any form of combat."

Without stating a reason, the draft board rejected John's appeal and reissued a new date for his induction. When he refused to show up a second time, he was arrested and eventually convicted in federal court of draft evasion. He was sentenced to three years of service in a mental hospital, fined $5,000, and placed on probation for five years. John appealed the decision to the Fourth Circuit of Appeals which, in April 1974, overturned the conviction on the grounds that the local draft board's failure to provide a reason for its rejection of conscientious objector claim deprived John of his right to administrative review and appeal of the board's decision. In commenting on the case, legal scholars viewed it as on course for U.S. Supreme Court review.

While my experience and John's were different in their outcomes, they originated and played out from the same dilemma arising from the loss of free will: the ability to make choices for oneself, independent of the decisions and influences of others.

So, who was the brave brother and who was the coward? Was I the brave one for accepting duty over personal desires. Or was John the courageous one for giving Uncle Sam the middle finger?

Epilogue. The O'Brien story and the stories of the Wainscott brothers make me ponder: what is courage? Is it gallantry—charging into danger without regard for one's safety? In other words, self-sacrifice? What is cowardice? Is it succumbing to societal pressures and taking the easy way out? Is it rejection of one's duty? Is it possible to be both courageous and cowardly?

Looking back on those times, I see my actions and decisions as neither courage nor cowardice, rather resignation to the inevitable. Yes, there was fear of being killed and having my body shipped back to my wife of less than a year. I was frequently haunted by thoughts of how I would perform in combat. Could I really pull the trigger on another human being? But even more emotionally troubling was the constant feeling of helplessness that came from realizing that I had absolutely no control over my destiny. The tension between duty and conscience goes on.

The Brink of Crazy

Chris Benson

Nineteen sixty-seven was the year my brother Mark—
two years older than I—and I spent a bucolic
summer on a farm in Iowa with my aunt and uncle. We
were city kids from the outskirts of Jersey City, just across
the Hudson River from Manhattan, and farm life was an
eye-opener. For the first time, I rode a tractor, swung on a
rope hung from a ridge pole in a barn, fed hogs in a pen,
gathered eggs from a chicken coop, and drank raw milk.
I also began, for the first time, to read a local newspaper
that was delivered each day to my aunt and uncle's house.
I leisurely spent my mornings on Aunt Ceil's living
room floor with the *Adams County Free Press* spread
out all around me, reading headlines, articles, want ads,
advertisements, and, of course, the comics. Many of the
articles were reprints of AP and UPI articles that covered
national and international news. That summer I read about
the riots going on in large cities all over the United States.
One city that got my attention was Newark, NJ, which was
close to where I lived.

The articles described inner-city looting, arson,
homicides, and general mayhem. At ten years old, I did
not understand the cause of the riots, but I gathered a
serious conflict existed between the Black populations

of these cities and the white Italians, Irish and Jews who governed them. Reporters attributed the unrest to chronic unemployment, inferior public housing, institutionalized police brutality, and other societal woes that were apparent to anyone with eyes to see. It would be another decade before I understood the complex social reasons for the riots of that summer, but I was, nonetheless, drawn to the graphic description of the violence of it during the time that came to be known as "The Long Hot Summer."

Ironically, there was much in the paper about it also being "The Summer of Love." *The Adams County Free Press* included an AP summary of the Monterey Pop Festival in June 1967, which included striking photos of young, strange-looking musicians and their fans who, though clearly not rioting, were in some kind of frenzied condition. These articles recounted something called a "Human Be-In"—whatever that was—and included photos of half-dressed hippies in loving embraces. These two events of 1967, the Summer of Love and the Long Hot Summer, seemed contradictory to me. How could it be a summer of love and hate?

Iowa pop radio was playing The Doors first big hit "Light My Fire," (1967) which was a love song, right? But there was more to it than that, something I couldn't identify yet felt nonetheless:

The time to hesitate is through;
no time to wallow in the mire;
try and we can only lose;
and our love become a funeral pyre
... try to set the night on fire.

I remained puzzled over the conflicting words and images I got from the newspaper and radio.

At end of summer, my brother and I returned to Jersey, and I started sixth grade at Saint Cecelia's Parish School.

I was not aware I had undergone any change that summer;
but looking back that was the year: I began to look at girls
differently. I learned sarcasm and cracked wise with my
21-year-old sister-in-law and delighted in making her howl
with laughter. I bullied a kid in my class during recess who
stood up to me with his fists and taught me a lesson. My
Catholic catechism workbook included a graphic drawing
of Russian Catholics being machine-gunned in the streets
by "the Communist government," and I knew instinctively
that the drawing was propaganda, even though that word
was not yet in my vocabulary. I grew self-conscious and
second-guessed my every word and action. Change was
afoot, but there was no epiphany for me that year. Instead,
it was a long year of puzzling through non-sequitur
experiences. Was I crazy or was sixth grade crazy?

When sixth grade was over, another summer loomed.
Each year Ma saved money to bring my brother and me
and our cousin Jackie to the shore for a week before
school started again. We always went to Seaside Park,
the southernmost town on the barrier strip of dunes that
protected Barnegat Bay from the Atlantic. The little town
was crammed with BENNYs, as the locals called the
lowbrow hordes who descended on Seaside each summer
from Bayonne, Elizabeth, Newark, New York, and every
other low-rent, working-class place in northern Jersey.
They came to rent rooms, apartments, and tiny ramshackle
cottages that were so close to each other you could hear
your neighbors arguing with each other through open
windows at night.

We could not afford an apartment close to the ocean, so
we had to walk two blocks on burning sidewalks, cross the
four-lane main drag, and walk two more blocks to get to the
beach. In August 1968, we rented an upstairs apartment of
a two-story house that was accessed by a wooden staircase
attached to the back of the house. At the top of the stairs,

a door opened into a small kitchen with one counter and a tiny oven. Past the kitchen was a living room with two lumpy daybeds and an RCA 26-inch black and white TV. When the beds were pulled out, there was no place to walk in the room. Down the hall from the living room were two bedrooms, one tiny one, where Ma slept, and one with two twin beds and a cot, where my brother, Jackie, and I slept.

Mark, Jackie, and I spent our entire day at the beach, rafting the waves on our canvas blow-ups. Ma would join us late in the morning, bringing buttered ham sandwiches for lunch. At the end of day, we were exhausted from swimming, paddling, fighting the waves, and holding our breath underwater. We'd drag ourselves home, rinse off with a garden hose below the wooden staircase, eat supper, and then flop on the two daybeds in front of the TV.

After supper, we would have preferred to watch reruns of *Get Smart* or *The Man from U.N.C.L.E.*, but Ma made us watch the Democratic Presidential Convention in Chicago. She was determined not to miss it. We didn't have the energy to argue with her or even retreat to our room to play Crazy Eights or Parchesi. We lay on the daybeds and watched the convention with blank expressions.

I knew the candidates Humphrey, Nixon, and Wallace from seeing them on TV news and from watching TV comedians do impersonations of them. My interest in politics went no further than that. But at the convention that week, riots broke out, and my interest was piqued, as it had been the previous summer by the Newark riots. But this was different; it was not Black people fighting white cops; it was young people, hippies both Black and White, fighting cops in sky-blue hardhats. It went on all week: one day, the rioting was in a city park where hundreds of hippies were camping. The next night it was in the streets outside the convention. Then it was on the floor inside the convention hall. The images were raw and immediate. The hippies didn't know how to fight back; one smack over the head with a billy club and they crumpled. To me, it looked like they were asking for it.

The whole country was going crazy over Vietnam. Why? Vietnam was just a war on the other side of the world against Chinese people. I'd never known a time when there was no such war. That was just the way it was. The whole country, including my brother and I, watched reruns of the war drama *Combat!* on TV. Everyone watched because the Americans always did the right thing and won.

After vacation at the shore, we returned home, and I faced seventh grade. That summer my cousin Timmy had flunked out of his first year of college, and Uncle Sam made him enlist in the Army. Now he was going to Vietnam. The nightly TV news continued that fall to show riots of young people protesting at colleges, and these news clips were mixed in with clips of U.S. soldiers in Vietnam in battle, who were the same age as the college students. These images were a regular diet at suppertime for our little family—Ma, Mark, and me. American soldiers fell where they were shot and were carried to helicopters. I never saw anybody die on camera, but I wondered if some soldiers died in those helicopters on the way to a hospital. Unlike the *Combat!* reruns, these scenes weren't scripted; there was real blood. When a camera focused on a soldier's face, he wasn't acting. I couldn't tell if the Americans were doing the right thing or winning. Our family fell silent at such times. I cleaned my plate and thought of cousin Timmy. I wondered if he could have been just offscreen.

Something changed during seventh grade for me. Part of it was that I was just getting older, and change was bound to come. A decade later in my twenties, I read the theories of Swiss psychologist Jean Piaget, who claimed a child's cognition naturally moves from concrete logic to abstract reasoning around age 12. Now, having raised a couple children of my own, I can see that I was, perhaps, merely maturing according to Piaget's theory. But I still wonder: was I seeing the world differently or was the world different? Was I crazy or was the world crazy?

My Summer of 1968

Susan Hilligoss

It was the biggest room I had ever seen. It could have
been a factory floor for building heavy equipment, with a
high ceiling and giant windows running down the side walls
to the end of the building. But instead of a production line
with conveyor belts and machine tools, it was filled with
rows and rows of metal filing cabinets. This was Records
Division, one floor of the 1.6 million square foot Finance
Center, U.S. Army, Fort Benjamin Harrison, located on the
northeast edge of Indianapolis.[1] The second largest office
building in the world, after the Pentagon, it was said.

I was a new GS-2 clerk, hired for the summer after my
sophomore year of college. I was against the Vietnam war
and had attended teach-ins and rallies on campus, along
with all of my friends. In March, while I was studying late
in the old graduate library stacks, I heard noises outside
on the Diag, the center of campus. I went to a window and
looked out into the dark, cold Michigan night. There was

---

[1] The Finance Center, U.S. Army (FCUSA) was relocated from Missouri to Indianapolis in
1950. https://www.usafmcom.army.mil/About-Us/History/
Accessed: August 15, 2025
Now known as "The Major General Emmett J. Bear Federal Center, commonly referred
to as Building One, is located in the northeast Indianapolis area (Lawrence, Ind.),
just a short distance outside the I-465 ring. This extraordinary structure includes 1.6
million square feet of federal space on 72 acres." Sources vary on the exact enclosed
space of the Pentagon.

a conga line of students chanting in jubilation. President
Lyndon Johnson, who escalated the war, had just announced
that he would not run for re-election. It was an eerie
moment. I can still see and hear that conga line, though I've
forgotten what they chanted.

When I took the civil service exam, I'd hoped for
an offer from the Social Security office in downtown
Indianapolis but knew that one of the big military
employers of civilians was more likely. I needed money to
stay in school, more than the $1.35 an hour the nice people
at my previous job had offered, a ten-cent raise. I didn't
have a car, and Fort Harrison was close to where my family
lived, so one of them could drop me off and pick me up.
Despite my nascent political beliefs, I decided to take the
offer to work there. It was late spring, 1968.

On that first day in Records Division, my escort, a slight
woman with gray-blond hair, maybe forty or so, led me to
an area that had about a dozen metal office desks in neat
rows, and gave me an empty one toward the back. She was
kind, and happy that her section had landed a summer hire
to help with the work. The full-time clerk who had had that
spot was not returning. I would rarely see the desk and chair
that summer, except to eat my bagged lunch.

Earlier that morning I had sat in a much smaller room on
a different floor, finishing my hiring paperwork under the
watchful eye of a supervisor. The room was empty except
for the two of us, although there was space for twenty or
more new hires. My college term finished early in May, so
I was among the first summer hires to arrive. What took
me the longest was reading, line by line, the giant list of
organizations that reportedly had ties to Communism. I had
to certify that I had never been a member of any of them.
"Be sure you read every one," the supervisor said, sensing
that I was speeding through too fast. So, I read every one. I
was nineteen, and most of the names struck me as foreign

and laughable, not to mention decades out of date. There was no Black Panther Party or Students for a Democratic Society. Instead, in tiny type was listed every Eastern European social club that had ever existed in America, every aid society for immigrants that could be tied to the Soviet bloc. From my stance as a sometime sociology student at the university where Students for a Democratic Society was created, I ironically pictured old guys with Polish names sitting together smoking after their shifts at an auto plant up in Detroit. The list had nothing to do with my life, but I read every line and remembered.

The job was simple. The Army was changing from military identification numbers to Social Security numbers. The summer hires were to relabel every active-duty soldier's financial records file folder by putting a computer-generated self-stick label over the old one. Very modern. There was more to it than that, of course. The war in Vietnam was at its most intense in 1968. President Johnson had called for troop levels to reach 549,000 in Vietnam. There were more soldiers, mainly draftees, than ever before.[2] Their pay records overwhelmed the civilian staff and threatened to burst out of the enormous space. In some areas of Records Division, the filing cabinets couldn't be closed because of the overflow of paper.[3] It took no time—a week, maybe—for me to put on the folder labels in our section. What I mainly did that summer was file huge stacks of backlogged pay records that we moved around on carts.

---

[2] "U.S. troop numbers peaked in 1968 with President Johnson approving an increased maximum number of U.S. troops in Vietnam at 549,500. The year was the most expensive in the Vietnam War with the American spending US$77.4 billion (US$ 603 billion in 2022) on the war. The year also became the deadliest of the Vietnam War for America and its allies..." https://en.wikipedia.org/wiki/1968_in_the_Vietnam_War Accessed: August 15, 2025

[3] A fascinating 1971 GAO report on poor Army finance record keeping and overpayments to separating service members says 750,000 separated in fiscal year 1970. https://www.gao.gov/assets/b-125037-095488.pdf Accessed: August 15, 2025

Our area, Section 5, covered last names M-Mc. Just M-Mc.

We worked alone in the alphabet ranges of cabinets.
I rarely saw the other staff members close enough to
chat with. I never saw another summer hire in the entire
division, although I didn't travel far outside our section.
Walking and standing seven-plus hours a day was enough.
In the long hours of filing, I amused myself in several ways.
One was noting the variety of soldiers' names. Often, they
seemed as foreign and laughable to my sardonic teenage
self as the list of banned organizations. I gave imaginary
awards for the oddest names or silently chanted the most
euphonious. It was petty and frivolous. It also impressed on
me the wide range of the soldiers' ethnicities. Polynesian
and Filipino names were especially interesting to me,
just because I'd never thought about them. Another way I
occupied myself was to imagine a history for the soldier
whose financial life I was trying to slide into his folder.
There might be "casual pay" receipts collected while the
soldier was in transit to postings. Small pink or yellow
slips were duplicates of claims filed by a dependent, likely
a wife. I held the basic 8x8-inch white, square pay record
and tried to visualize a company clerk typing it in Southeast
Asia. I held something in my hand that might have traveled
thousands of miles from a war zone.

The women who worked in Section 5 were close and
often ate lunch together. I sometimes joined them rather
than eat at my desk. The gray-blond woman who trained
me had a son in the military, as did most of the others. I was
the same age as their children. I just listened. I was the only
college student most of them knew. They were patriotic
and proud of their sons' service, but also realistic, maybe
fatalistic, about the prospect that their children might not
come home. They took their jobs seriously. Like me, they
knew that the federal government had the best paying
jobs for women without specialized skills. They were all

white. The civil service is integrated, and Records Division certainly was, but smaller employee groups tended to be segregated.

I had been working there for about a month when I came in to find most of the Section 5 staff milling about near the desk area, some talking, some just standing. No one was loading carts or headed into the cabinet rows. They were upset. It was the morning of June 5. Senator Robert F. Kennedy had been assassinated shortly after midnight the night before, in a Los Angeles hotel, after winning the California presidential primary. They were in shock. They didn't know what to do, how to get back to work, these women who were so focused on doing their jobs well and on time. My trainer and mentor showed me the framed photo of Bobby, as she called him, on her desk, there with her family photos. I looked around and realized hers wasn't the only one. Other desks honored him as well. I hadn't paid attention. I didn't get it, why this reverence. "He had just been here," I heard someone say. Yes, I knew that vaguely. He had made a campaign stop in Indianapolis, before I got home from college. I was in exams. I wasn't old enough to vote. I wasn't paying attention then, either. But in the ensuing years, I started to.

Senator Kennedy had been in Indianapolis on April 4, the day Martin Luther King, Jr., was assassinated. Years later, I learned that Kennedy had made three stops in Indiana that day. The third and last was in Indianapolis, after hearing of King's death on the flight from Muncie. Indianapolis Mayor Richard Lugar recommended canceling the evening appearance, but Senator Kennedy insisted. He gave a memorable and often quoted speech to a mainly Black audience assembled in Broadway Park.

These were his words, as reported in the *Indianapolis Star*: "I have bad news for you," he began, "...for all fellow citizens, and people who love peace all over the world, and that is that Dr. Martin Luther King was shot and killed tonight...Martin Luther King dedicated his life to love and to justice for his fellow human beings, and he died in the cause of that effort. For those of you who are black, considering the evidence that there evidently were white people who were responsible, you can be filled with bitterness, with hatred and a desire for revenge. We can move in that direction as a country, in great polarization... Or we can make an effort, as Martin Luther King did, to understand and to comprehend, and to replace that violence, that stain of bloodshed that has spread across our land, with an effort to understand with compassion and love."[4]

I have no idea if any of the women I worked with were at that April rally. I do not know what any of them thought about Martin Luther King, Jr. I suspect they did not revere him. They did not discuss civil rights. They weren't activists. I do know that they saw Bobby Kennedy as a champion and an ally for them, for their children, for all Americans, especially the poor. We went back to work filing.

Two months later I returned to college. In late August the anti-war movement became forever allied with violence at the Democratic convention in Chicago. Over months and years, I started to connect the war in Vietnam with the daily lives of the men and women who served there or served anywhere else in the U.S. military. Most important, I began, slowly, to connect the war with the experiences of women and men who were unlike me and who lived out the policies—the military draft, the GI Bill, Civil Rights, the fight for equal pay and treatment, the complex political reality in which everyday people made life and death choices—the policies that Washington leaders put into place along with authorizing funds for war. I went back to Fort

[4] Indiana and Indianapolis accounts of RFK's itinerary and visit on April 4, 1968 https://images.indianahistory.org/digital/collection/dc019/search Accessed: August 15, 2025

Harrison in the summers of 1969 and 1970. Before working for the Army, I had been against the Vietnam War, and that never changed. But I was starting to understand what to be for.

U.S. Army UH-1H Hueys insert ARVN troops at Khâm Đúc, Vietnam, 12 July 1970.

U.S. Air Force (Operation Holly 1970 (Folder 13 of 15), sheet 182), Public domain, via Wikimedia Commons: https://commons.wikimedia.org/wiki/File:U.S._Army_UH-1H_Hueys_insert_ARVN_ troops_at_Kh%C3%A2m_%C4%90%E1%BB%A9c,_Vietnam,_12_July_1970_ (79431435).jpg

Accessed September 21, 2025

Vietnam: Two Stories

Debra Broadwell Jackson

From college to war. The Vietnam War started on
November 1, 1955, but major changes occurred
in 1964 after the Gulf of Tonkin incident which expanded
the deployment of troops into Vietnam in 1965. I was a
high school sophomore. My brother graduated from high
school that May. The draft lottery for determining the order
of conscription was initiated in December 1969. These
dates stand out for me because of the implementation and
implication of the lottery and how it affected my friends
from 1969 through June of 1973.

During high school, three of us (Nancy, Sally, and I)
were always together. We had a friend, Andy, who was part
of our group as well. Andy was a year ahead of us in school
and turned 18 a year before we did. Eighteen was a magical
age to be. It meant you could buy beer and wine! Andy
could and did provide us with them. The wine was awful,
mainly because it was cheap, not to mention we usually
had to push the cork into the bottle because we never
had a corkscrew. We spent our high school years playing
miniature golf, going to movies, and just hanging out. The
four of us went to four different colleges but stayed in
touch with regular letters, visits to see each other, weddings
(Nancy and Sally), and holidays. Nancy was the best

correspondent. I loved her letters, which I enthusiastically opened throughout my college years. Have you ever known a person who would rather tell a story, that is, lie or exaggerate, than tell the truth? Nancy's stories in person and in writing were descriptive, interesting, and much more exciting than my life. I was eager to believe every word.

The four of us spent holidays together during our college years. Once Nancy and Sally married, Andy and I were the last two left to continue our hometown traditions. Until I married, Andy and I continued to visit and spend time together. Our favorite tradition was Christmas Day, after time with our families, we went to the movies, a tradition that lasted years. We lived less than a mile from each other growing up, and when Andy was in Atlanta, he stayed at my place. He was a second brother and a good friend.

In 1969, the Vietnam draft lottery meant that all young men knew when they might be called up for Vietnam. They did have options for deferments: current enrollment in college, conscientious objector status, and medical exemptions. My brother, Michael, ended up with a medical exemption for his juvenile onset glaucoma which showed up as he enrolled in graduate school. My brother was an active protester against the Vietnam War. I was in Charleston dating Citadel cadets, all of whom expected to go to Vietnam as they graduated.

It was different with a friend who really did not plan to serve in the military. Andy was not as lucky as my brother. As he completed college in 1970, his "number" was coming up, and he had a decision to make: his only choice was to enlist in a military service and hope to be assigned anywhere but Vietnam.

Andy chose the Army and worked with his recruiting officer to enroll in the German Language program. After a year of training, he would be assigned to Germany. It sounded like a great plan. The only issue was that rather than German Language school, Andy was sent to a yearlong Vietnamese Language program.

I graduated from college in 1971 and moved to Atlanta. Andy completed his training and was ready to deploy to Vietnam in 1972. I do not remember how Andy arrived in Atlanta, but he did and stayed with my roommates and me for one night. The next morning, I drove him to the Atlanta airport and put him on the flight that would ultimately take him to Vietnam. I parked the car, walked him to his gate, and stayed until the plane left. The evening before Andy had given me a book to read: *Johnny Got His Gun* by Dalton Trumbo. Published in 1939, this anti-war novel tells the story of a young man, Joe, whose horrifying injuries sustained in WWI include the loss of both arms, legs, eyes, ears, teeth, and tongue. His only movement is his head. He can feel warmth, a touch, and eventually Joe learns to communicates through Morse code. However, it takes time, and a nurse recognizes that Joe is conscious and responds to touch, and that he is communicating. Publication of the book was suppressed during WWII but later gained greater recognition during the Vietnam era and was made into a movie in 1971. In view of its harrowing theme of war and suffering, it is not a novel to read as one goes off to war.

Throughout Andy's time in Vietnam, we communicated through letters. Nancy and Sally were in touch with him as well. In one of his first letters to me, he told me about spending his first night in the barracks, being issued his gun, but no bullets. When the unit came under fire, he had no way to defend himself. His job was in communications, and he never talked about the details of the role he played and the dangers he experienced.

When his tour was completed, I picked up Andy at the Atlanta airport. By this time, Nancy was divorced, and she and I were roommates in Atlanta. Was he different on his return? Yes. Andy was always quiet, but he changed the subject when we asked about his Vietnam experiences. No one thanked Andy for his service when he returned in 1974. I was not surprised he did not talk about this time in Vietnam. At that time, I was working at the Veterans Administration Hospital in Atlanta. I knew from my patients how awful the war was for soldiers. My father never spoke about his time in the Pacific in World War II until he was in his late sixties. Perhaps it takes time to process the horrible things you see and experience. Perhaps Andy did not think he made a difference by being in Vietnam. The public outcries and protests about Vietnam would have had an effect on his reticence as well.

Andy was glad to be in civilian clothes and able to avoid questions. He had started drinking more than before Vietnam and perhaps smoking pot. He found a job in Columbia and was happy enough but had no regular girlfriend. Andy was a regular visitor with us in Atlanta. I thought he and Nancy would become an item, but that did not happen. Nancy married (again) and moved. Andy continued to visit and stayed over in Atlanta and joined me for a movie on Christmas night in Anderson. Andy married and had a daughter and moved across the country. We do not talk anymore, but Andy, Sally and I are Facebook "friends." Andy posts on Facebook with his Army buddies from time to time. Perhaps in 2025, it is okay to be a veteran.

The long-term consequences and reality of war. During college in Charleston (1967-1971), I learned a lot about young men in the military and dated Citadel cadets. Most of them would be commissioned officers in one of the armed services on graduation and shortly afterwards be sent to Vietnam. Furthermore, in our nursing program, we did our psychiatric nursing course work at the Veterans Administration Hospital in Charleston. Our assigned patients were young men who had returned from Vietnam and were suffering from symptoms of Post-Traumatic Stress Disorder (PTSD). Unfortunately, PTSD was not considered a mental health diagnosis until 1980, stemming from research primarily with Vietnam war veterans.

I had many wonderful opportunities throughout my career and one of my most memorable was time spent at the VA Hospital in Atlanta. I was teaching an eight-week non-degree certification program for Registered Nurses, in wounds, ostomy, and continence nursing (WOCN). Students in this program were assigned clinical experiences in all the major hospital settings in Atlanta, such as Emory University Hospital, Grady Memorial, the VA Hospital of Atlanta, Egleston Children's Hospital, Piedmont Hospital, Northside Hospital, and several out-patient clinics, as well.

In Vietnam, the mortality rate was 10% if a wounded soldier made it to a field hospital. The process of triage, i.e., sorting the speed and delivery of care according to the severity of the injury, enabled doctors, medics, and nurses to work together efficiently and save many lives. Most veteran deaths were related to abdominal wounds, hemorrhage, sepsis, and pulmonary failure related to shock. At the VA Hospital in Atlanta, we were to care for the wounded who made it home.

From 1974 to 1983, I spent every Wednesday at the VA Hospital, where I saw the devastating effects of war. Veterans from World War II and Vietnam were seen in the outpatient clinics and in the hospital rooms. Their injuries varied from missing limbs to paralysis to PTSD. The wounds we saw were heartbreaking. A patient might be hospitalized for weeks to months, and families were not able to stay and help. The waiting time for the clinic appointments hindered the progress of excellent and compassionate care provided by nurses and doctors. The scope and nature of the injuries overwhelmed the veterans and their families and those caring for them.

Each institution where I placed students for clinical experiences had a nurse who was WOCN certified. We did not pay our clinical faculty; they donated their time and efforts to the program. I went to a different hospital each day of the week both to show my support and commitment to the clinical faculty members' efforts, but also to help with patient care, and evaluate the students. Edith Sikes was the contact person at the VA. When I spoke with Edith about which day she would like me to be at the VA, she recommended Wednesday (it was fried chicken day in the cafeteria). She was right, it was the best day to be at the VA.

Edith Sikes was the most generous person I knew, and she cared deeply for the veterans with whom she worked. She saw her patients in their rooms, in an out-patient clinic, and in her office. Edith was a joy, and a very dear friend. The young and old men that were admitted spent weeks, not days at the VA Hospital. She found ways to help the veterans find something unique to do each week. We would take patients to the patio and have picnics. Arby's coupons were available, so you might purchase ten sandwiches for $5. We never let a coupon go to waste. We would roll wheelchairs and stretchers outside for an hour. I did feel bad when we allowed one young man to get a mild sunburn.

I learned more about living with amputations, paralysis, venous leg ulcers, pressure sores and erectile dysfunction from the men seen over these years. *Johnny Got His Gun* may have introduced me to the horror of wars, but the VA Hospital showed me firsthand the experiences and the long-term consequences of war on people injured physically and psychologically by war.

Medical science has come far since 1983, such as the improvement of prosthetic limbs which are now highly specialized, lightweight, high-performing, and motorized.

Moreover, the use of sensors and microprocesses have improved the lives of so many. During the last 40 years, advances in medicine related to war injuries have included use of one-handed tourniquets, battlefield dressings infused with the blood-clotting protein fibrin, hemostatic devices like XStat which injects small rapidly-expanding sponges into a rapidly bleeding injury, pain management that reduces pain without sedation, biomarkers for traumatic brain injury, burn repair, regenerative medicine to reduce scarring, and reconstructive surgery. PTSD remains a critical injury, but therapies are available. Plus, the public's attitude toward military service has vastly improved since the Vietnam era, and we not only celebrate veterans' service but also thank them and provide everything we can to compensate them for their sacrifices.

Vietnam War Memorial, Washington, DC
(Maya Lin)

The Only Sane Man

Chris Benson

In 1968, my cousin Timmy was put on academic
probation at the end of his first year at Ohio State
University, and returned home to his parents' house in
Elizabeth, New Jersey. His father, my Uncle Sam, said,
"Looks like it's the army now." Uncle Sam had served
in the military in WWII, like most of my uncles. But by
1968 that was ancient history, and none of my uncles now
remotely resembled their younger selves who fought in
Europe or the Pacific. In middle age and pushing fifty
or better, they were old men in my eyes, almost another
species. I didn't get to see Timmy off to Vietnam, not that I
would have asked to. He was probably nineteen, and I was
twelve, and we had little in common except the fact that our
mothers were sisters.

When Timmy was in Vietnam, Ma used to send him
care packages of goodies. She kept a cardboard shoebox
on our attic stairs and over several weeks filled it with
peanut butter crackers, M&Ms, Mars and O'Henry candy
bars, TastyKakes, and miniature pies in cellophane that
you could buy anywhere in New Jersey for twenty cents.
When the box was full of goodies, she mailed it overseas
to Timmy and started another box. I envied Timmy in the
army getting those care packages of treats that we never

got at home. Ma kept a sharp eye on Timmy's box and hid it from us in different places. I found it and robbed it a few times, once discovering it in the shed out back, like treasure stashed in a cave.

Timmy must have got an honorable discharge, but all my cousins thought something happened to Timmy over there. After he'd been home for some time, his parents, Aunt Ellen and Uncle Sam, were at their wits' end with him. He had trouble keeping a job, slept upstairs a lot while Uncle Sam slept downstairs until it was time for him to go to work at the *Star-Ledger*, a morning newspaper out of Newark. Uncle Sam, my favorite uncle and my godfather, was blue collar all the way; he probably loaded bundles of the *Ledger* into trucks or drove the trucks to drop off points. Every day sometime after noon, Timmy ventured downstairs, doing an evening reconnaissance of the household to make sure his father was gone. He sometimes provoked the family in some way at supper before disappearing into the night. He'd often say strange or disturbing things, and it was hard to understand where he was coming from. News of his remarks or stunts traveled like electricity through our extended family of aunts, uncles, and cousins. "Did you hear what Timmy did!"

It wasn't long before Timmy left his parents' house. Timmy lived at first on a series of couches, including that of my older brother Rich, who was a few years older than Timmy and already married. Timmy returned to his parents' house frequently where Aunt Ellen fed him and tried to talk some sense into him. He got her hopes up, promising to make changes, but then she'd learn something the next day that brought it all back to square one. Once he'd got into trouble in a pet store for releasing parakeets from their cage. It seemed a crazy thing to do, but on the other hand, a compassionate love of animals must have motivated the act.

No one ever pressed charges against Timmy for anything; there was nothing to be gained by doing so.

A couple of my older cousins claimed Timmy had got messed up on LSD in college, and, of course, worse things happened in Vietnam. But nobody knew exactly what happened to Timmy that set him off. I was only twelve years old but smart enough to prick up my ears at such information, especially in conversations between Ma and her younger sister Ellen, who frequently called our house with worries over Timmy. Ma sat in the recliner with the phone pressed to her ear. The receiver had a long cord attached to the wall phone in the kitchen so it could reach into the family room where the TV was. In the evenings, I lay on the couch next to Ma's recliner watching *I Love Lucy* or *I Dream of Jeannie* reruns and overheard her half of the conversation with Ellen. That was all I needed to hear to know that Timmy could be frustrating, even disturbing. At our big family get-togethers in those days, with a dozen aunts and uncles and fifteen or twenty cousins, I avoided Timmy because he scared me a little, and I offered only a quick hello before joining my other cousins playing board games or watching TV.

Timmy's eyes were wide with a lot of white showing, as if he could see things others could not. He never shared any insights with me, but, then, I kept my distance, too. His eyes seemed to be searching for something, but as a tweener, I was afraid to ask what, even though it might be brilliant and fascinating. Indeed, Timmy appeared to be the picture of a sage or guru—with hollowed cheeks, long lank hair and a long beard. Timmy spoke with an intense emphasis, and his words seemed to hint at cosmic secrets, though expressed in statements as unsettling as they were mysterious.

Shortly after Timmy came home from Vietnam, our large family gathered at our house for Christmas, and all our aunts and uncles and cousins piled into our little salt box house for the celebration. Our house was so small we had to spread out and gather in every room in order for all of us to fit, including the bedrooms and the unfinished basement, where most of the family gathered. Downstairs, Uncle Bill and Uncle Jim were dipping whisky sours out of the punch bowl on the washing machine and discussing Nixon's doings. Aunt Agatha and Aunt Maureen were trading Christmas cookie recipes over by the sump pump.

For Christmas that year I had got an amateur reel-to-reel tape recorder, about the size of a cigar box. This was before cassette tapes were on the market, and the gift was a novelty. Timmy spent most of that Christmas afternoon playing with the device in my bedroom and recording himself. That night, after everyone was gone, I found Timmy's opus on the reel to reel, all five minutes of it consisting of two statements over and over again: "Silence is golden. Golden is silence. Silence is golden. Golden is silence." In my pajamas, I lay on my bed in the dark listening to it, expecting the recitation to develop into something else, but that was it: "Silence is golden. Golden is silence." I kept listening. Two minutes into it, I was transported somewhere metaphysically. I pretended as I lay there listening to Timmy's voice that I was on an LSD trip. Later, I let my brother Mark listen to it. He listened to about thirty seconds before he snapped it off and gave it a concise review, "Timmy's fucking crazy."

Like most hippies at the time, Timmy dressed the part in tattered jeans and his old green army field jacket. A lot of the time we didn't know where he was. He dropped in at his parents' house, but the visits became less frequent as he found a series of apartments and places to stay. Over the months, I gathered from the phone conversations that Ma had with Aunt Ellen that Timmy had done something bizarre, like the parakeet episode. We'd laugh—albeit nervously—and say, "Timmy! What a card!" But other times his actions were not amusing. He borrowed my brother's car for an afternoon and disappeared for a whole night. My brother wasn't in a forgiving mood when the car was returned. Another time, Timmy was discovered one night in the wee hours sleeping in a random stranger's car on the street. Aunt Ellen clung to the hope that he'd snap out of it, and she prayed hard for Timmy.

Ma managed to convince Ellen that the Veterans Administration could help, and they got him admitted. This moment initiated a relationship between my mother and Timmy that was very sweet and loving. Timmy was diagnosed with schizophrenia. He was prescribed antipsychotics that helped some, but treating schizophrenia with antipsychotics in the early 1970s was hit or miss, like shooting at a fly with a blunderbuss. Doctors did not yet know much about schizophrenia, let alone PTSD, which hadn't been "invented" yet. You had to believe antipsychotics worked for them to actually work.

Timmy began a period of life when he would be admitted to the VA, receive medicine for schizophrenia, get better, be released and then go off the medicine because of the side effects. Without the medicine, his condition would deteriorate, and he'd repeat the cycle.

For a brief time, Timmy stayed with my brother Mark, who was working his first professional job as a high school math teacher. One day Mark came home from school and found Timmy had graded a stack of algebra quizzes my brother had left on the kitchen table. Timmy graded them using some kind of personal hieroglyphics. In addition, he'd scrawled in red pen on some of the quizzes, "I AM JESUS CHRIST!!" My brother laughed this off, later telling his students he'd lost the quizzes and was giving them all "A's" on it.

Another time, my brother had his girlfriend sleep over. Timmy was on the couch as usual. The next morning my brother woke up to find Timmy standing in my brother's bedroom doorway looking at the girlfriend who lay sleeping, naked from the waist up. Even this was too much for my tolerant brother. Timmy had to go.

When I was a sophomore in college at Coby in upstate New York, I hitchhiked home for Easter with my dog, Rex. I saw Timmy at the big family get-together on Easter Sunday. When Timmy found out I had no ride back to college and would have to take a bus or hitchhike, he immediately volunteered to take me and Rex back. That was just like Timmy: he was spontaneous and unpredictable, but also kindhearted, generous, and loving. The following Sunday, he drove me and my dog in his sporty red VW with the black-and-white checkered seats five hours upstate. He planned to spend a few days with me in the farmhouse I rented with my girlfriend Carolyn and our roommate Rick.

The trip upstate went fine. At this time, Timmy was prospering, holding down a job and saving money. Timmy probably had little experience in rural areas because he was very excited to see the countryside with all the old barns and fields of Holstein cows. At the farmhouse, we shared a couple good days and many homecooked meals together. I went to classes and hurried home to make sure Timmy was okay, and there he was sitting placidly on the couch reading a magazine or watching TV. For all I knew, he was completely cured of his schizophrenia.

The third day of his visit at the farm was the first clear warm, sunny day of spring, and I came home from school to find a note from Timmy. "Took Rex for a walk. Be back later." This didn't alarm me; it was only three p.m. But by six the sun was setting, and I was anxious. I walked out my driveway and went a half mile down the gravel road in one direction; then turned around and walked the opposite way, yelling at the top of my lungs for Timmy and Rex. No answer.

By seven, I was pacing the kitchen wondering what to do. Call my mother? Call my brother? What could they do from 250 miles away? I heard a noise at the door. Thank God! Feeling a weight slip from my shoulders, I ran to the door ready to unload on Timmy, but it was only Rex.

I gave Rex some water and interrogated him. "Where's Timmy, Rex?"

No answer. Not a trace of understanding in his grateful brown eyes. I took Rex to the door and let him out on the steps. "Where's Timmy, Rex?" I was hoping for a Lassie moment. A cool wind was blowing steady. The hills of upstate New York could get very cold in early April. Rex and I peered dumbly into the darkness.

An hour later, the side door opened, and Timmy fell into the kitchen looking like he'd been hounded by demons. He was panting with anxiety. I was, too. He'd left the house at 2 p.m. for a sunny walk, barefoot. He'd been lost in the woods and on rural unpaved roads for seven hours. His feet were muddy, blistered, and bruised.

I was so glad to see him in one piece that I couldn't be mad at him. But the next day I blew off my morning classes and helped Timmy leave. I insisted. I carried his duffel bag to his VW, put it and him in the car, and made sure he pulled out of my driveway headed in the right direction: out of my jurisdiction. Timmy was crazy but thank God he was not my crazy.

Timmy did his best to get better under therapy from the VA doctors, but the side effects of the medication sometimes seemed worse than the condition itself. Timmy cycled through a series of on-again/off-again medicated periods until two things happened: first, the medicine and the physicians' treatment improved during the eighties, and, second, Timmy was able to accept the medicine as a necessary inevitability, a significant accomplishment for him. Eventually, Timmy registered in a group home, the first in a series that would house him for the rest of his life.

In the nineties, Timmy ended up in Asbury Park, NJ, which had been a gorgeous seaside resort in the first half of the twentieth century but by the late 1980s was down at the heels and badly so. The grand old hotels had shuttered windows and broken porch railings; their paint was peeling off in sheets, and their signs were missing letters. The majestic art-deco Baronet Theatre, built in the early part of the century, now ran porn sixteen hours a day.

Many of Asbury's large stately homes that had been owned by generations of the affluent class had been converted into group homes with mini-apartments where society's unfortunate—the chronically addicted, mentally disabled, and mentally ill—came to live. Timmy came to rest in one such group home in Asbury, growing his yellow fingernails perversely long, going bald on top while letting his gray hair on the sides grow long and stringy, and smoking generic nonfiltered cigarettes into the wee hours. During these last ten or fifteen years, Timmy seemed to have made his peace. My mother lived in the adjacent town of Monmouth Beach and visited him, driving him places he needed to go and giving him food and little gifts just as she had when he was in Vietnam.

For years I marveled at the close relationship that Timmy and my mother enjoyed. I don't know of an aunt and nephew who were as fond of each other as they were. They had a dear relationship.

While I was visiting my mother in the summer of 2001, she invited Timmy over to visit. She picked him up and we had lunch together at her house. Timmy and I had not seen each other in years. After lunch, we sat on the side porch and talked. Timmy still spoke directly from his heart, unselfish in spirit and with great honesty. He was curious to know what I was doing and what I was thinking. He knew the names of my two children and asked about them. Our conversation drifted to the subject of writing. I knew he had been a gifted writer when he was in high school and asked if he wrote anything now. He got a crestfallen look on his face and shook his head. That was in the past. But he was very interested in my writing and asked enthusiastically about my recent book of poems. I later mailed him a copy of the book.

In September 2003, I was saddened to hear from my mother that Timmy died peacefully in his sleep, probably from emphysema or heart disease from smoking. Timmy's younger sister Shelley, whom he stayed close to throughout his life, contacted me after she had removed his effects from his apartment in the group home. She wanted to tell me she'd found my book of poems in the drawer of Timmy's night table.

In the Nineties, as new drugs were being developed to supplant the first generation of hit-or-miss antipsychotic drugs for schizophrenics, studies began to show, curiously, that schizophrenia was significantly more common in the U.S. than in Europe. Some psychiatrists pointed to possible social causes of the condition. Some went as far as to suggest that schizophrenics were actually sane people living in an insane world. My cousin Timmy lived on the border between a sane world and an insane one, between funny crazy and scary crazy. Something may have happened to Timmy "over there" in Vietnam, but no one ever discovered what. Perhaps the insanity of the world was revealed to him there. He was never the same after it. When Timmy died in his early 50s, he may have been the only sane man left in an insane world.

Jane Fonda and Donald Sutherland in the FTA Show, 1971

Jane Fonda Comes to Kenyon College

Marty Duckenfield

Ever since my college days of listening to folk music like "Blowin' in the Wind," I had been opposed to the Vietnam War. As a seventh-grade teacher in 1968, I invited to the classroom a cousin of one of my students to talk about his recent experience in Vietnam. He had been a telephone linesman behind the lines, and the boys in the class were disappointed he hadn't been in a foxhole with a gun. Trying to broaden their perspectives had been my goal, but at 22 I was too young to realize they were too young. Even so, my own perspectives were gradually being broadened.

Following my brief two-year teaching experience, my husband Chris and I relocated to England, which separated me from the constant news of the war; navigating a new culture and the novel experience of motherhood was enough to keep me occupied. Yet when Kent State happened, I was stunned. That news quickly made its way across the Atlantic to be the headline story of both the *Guardian* and *BBC News*, and the fact that four students had been killed revitalized my feelings of dismay with the ongoing war.

After we ended up at Kenyon College, in the fall of 1972 I learned that the students were hosting Jane Fonda, and my need to attend was compelling. My prior experience with rallies dated back to the presidential campaign of 1968 and going to see Eugene McCarthy, clearly antiwar and persuasive but hardly dynamic.

By contrast, my experience on the day of Fonda's visit over four years later was riveting.

Before I left the house, I made a tuna noodle casserole in the crockpot, so it would be ready whenever anyone was hungry, and so I could stay till the conclusion of the event. With my evening duties performed, I was ready to go when Chris came home early to oversee the boys. If I was late, they could at least eat!

With great anticipation, I arrived at the fieldhouse, which housed the basketball games and track events in winter. It was filling up, mostly with students, and a capacity crowd of hundreds awaited the anti-war event. Jane Fonda's husband, Tom Hayden, the well-known political and civil rights activist, led the program with his own remarks followed by two Vietnam vets. The vets were much more eloquent than the telephone linesman, for they had returned hardened in their opposition to the war, which animated their telling of their experiences. Their stories were about a reality seldom heard, and I could tell I was as one with the students' feelings of horror. The veterans effectively played the role of the warm-up crew for Jane Fonda.

Like the crowd, I was totally immersed in this heightened atmosphere of emotion. As promised, out came Jane Fonda, the main event. She was deeply against the war, and, having become an activist, her passion and acting skills made her extremely eloquent. As much as the others had touched my conscience, Jane finished the job by mesmerizing me and the mostly sympathetic members of the crowd. She spoke for the longest time of any speaker

I had ever heard; I learned later that the cost to the student lecture association was just $300. They got their money's worth!

We sat in the bleachers for hours, neither noticing the hard seats nor the time passing, and when it ended, the crowd was quiet, as if in a trance. Suddenly, reality reappeared. Tired and hungry, the students returned to their dorms and the cafeteria. For my part, hungry but full of stories to share with Chris, I hurried home to a restorative meal of tuna noodle casserole. It was perfect.

Jane Fonda's appearance at Kenyon took place just a few weeks before the 1972 presidential election of Richard Nixon who claimed he had a plan to end the war. Nevertheless, in my way of thinking, the man who had been honestly anti-war from the start was George McGovern, and so he got my vote.

Reflections at the Traveling Vietnam Veterans Memorial, Clemson, SC, November 14, 2008

With permission of photographer, Delbert L. Kimbler, Professor Emeritus of Industrial Engineering

My Long Relationship with Vietnam

Kenneth Steven Marsh

Our tight group of four guys graduated from high school in 1964 and represented each available choice regarding the Vietnam War. Ed enlisted in the Air Force, John was drafted into the Army, Cliff enlisted in the Marines, and I was deferred. John would never talk about any of his experiences in the Army. Cliff was keyed into the excitement or adrenaline of war in a way that I really couldn't understand. He was my best friend before he went in, but we got to the point where we didn't communicate. He re-upped three times, and he was killed on Hill 881 in 1967. I have viewed his name on the black wall that is the Vietnam Monument and performed the rubbings.

I entered college (with a deferment) with the intent to be a physics major. Freshmen registered last at Adelphi University, and I was closed out of first semester physics, so I signed up for chemistry. I declared myself an undecided major, a designation that gave me a lot more flexibility in choosing courses. Since I planned to be starting a physics major in my second year, that major for me would amount to a five-year program, keeping me out of the draft for that period. The draft board had installed a lottery system, renewed yearly, through which those with birthdays with lower numbers were drafted first. By 1968 the Vietnam War was in full swing, and New York draft boards were looking for draftees so one's lottery number was a significant concern. The draft lottery is always a gamble, but for graduation, I had a choice between two years: 1968, if I majored in chemistry, and 1969, if I majored in physics.

I was an active protester against the war. I believe diplomacy should be used more and conflict less. I was never against the soldiers but rather those who sent them halfway around the world. I protested at small events at Adelphi, and a few major ones: two in Washington, D.C., and two in New York City. There was an interesting contrast between the two locations. The New York police were present to keep the march safe and manageable— clearly separating groups of divergent opinion. In one minor incident, protesters were getting heckled by a group making verbal threats. I whispered to those on either side of me to pass down a message and on my signal some 60 of us turned towards them and hollered, "THE HECK WITH THIS PEACE JAZZ, LET'S GET THEM!" The police were not within earshot. The antagonistic group chose to depart quickly—but in truth there was little threat of a physical conflict.

Washington, D.C. was quite different. We had a totally peaceful march with about 100,000 people. An earlier march in D.C. was just completing while a second was assembling at the Pentagon, and the bulk of the earlier marchers was starting to leave. I was on the Mall about sixty feet from the place where a helicopter flying low tipped a cannister out its hatch that hit the ground and exploded with tear gas. Tear gas is nasty stuff and can elicit very angry responses. My girlfriend at the time was a peacenik, and also a brown belt in Aikido. She was so angry that I made sure we did not encounter any D.C. police because she was not in a cooperative mood. It occurred to me that a government that wishes to preserve its war effort does not want peaceful protests. They much prefer conflicts to demonstrate that protesters are violent people.

I ended up graduating in four years as an undecided major (the only graduate from Adelphi at that time with that status) with almost twice the credits required for a chemistry major, one course shy of a physics major, and two courses shy of a math major. That put me in good stead for the future—but I still had to fight the draft.

At the time, NYC had a teacher shortage and, consequently, developed a program at Hunter College in which students would take its Intensive Teacher Training program at his or her expense, and Hunter guaranteed a teaching job and (at least the men) a draft deferment. The program was very popular for these reasons. I enrolled and completed the program, confident that I would not have to join my friend Cliff. However, NYC later admitted they'd overenrolled by 2,000 people and basically said, "Oops, sorry." So, I found myself at the end of the summer with no job, no money, and the draft breathing down my neck. But a rescue in the form of a suitable offer came up as a result of a professor I had impressed during my freshman chemistry class at Adelphi.

On my first day at Adelphi, Professor Dwyer, a chemistry professor, had set up a demonstration of a "beating blob," a drop of mercury in an acid oxidizing solution with a radial conductor that would "beat" by cycling between a more spherical and more squashed state. Dr. Dwyer said the cause was unknown, and if anyone could provide an explanation, he/she would get an "A." I took the challenge and worked on it in the lab. But I didn't find the answer. After a semester, I moved on but did come up with an explanation a couple of years later and presented it to Dr. He nodded and said, "I owe you an "A.""

Well, Dr. Dwyer had left Adelphi and was currently setting up a graduate chemistry program at C.W. Post College of Long Island University. He asked me to help him establish the program with research publications, and in exchange he would write a letter stating my research was essential to the war effort. I was, after all, working on high-energy plasmas that could have eventually had a military application but surely not a critical or urgent one. Once again, I was in a deferred position regarding the draft. I completed two years and sufficient course work for a masters in Dr. Dwyer's lab.

I was successful with avoiding the draft and any association with the Vietnam War. Years later, however, before and after my time at Clemson, I became acquainted with Vietnam and some of its people. I befriended a Vietnamese couple in the U.S. and visited them in Vietnam when I accepted an invitation to speak at a symposium in Ho Chi Minh City (formerly Saigon). At the symposium. I befriended Dr. Luu Dzuan, a vice-president, professor and part owner of Saigon University and returned to Vietnam for another symposium and two visits as a visiting professor through the Vietnam Association of Food Science and Technology (VAFoST). Despite my ardor in avoiding Vietnam in the Sixties, fate and destiny was determined to make sure I got there.

A conversation I heard between a U.S. Vietnam vet and Vietnamese man is worth repeating. The vet had returned to Vietnam to visit decades after the war. The gentleman from Vietnam was very friendly to the former soldier, who asked, "How can you be so friendly, since we were former enemies?" The gentleman smiled, "The Chinese have beat on us for 2,000 years. You guys were a passing annoyance." I also have experienced the friendliness and hospitality of the Vietnamese. When I met Dr. Dzuan from Saigon University at a World Food Congress in Brazil, he came over and gave me a hug as if we had known each other for 30 years—and it felt absolutely spontaneous and natural.

More important, I am a very proud grandfather to two Vietnamese grandsons: one teaching physics in New York City and one getting ready to enter college as I write this. Moreover, Vietnam played a part in many of my friends' lives. My good friend and sailing buddy, John Gale, was a marine in Vietnam and piloted helicopters commanded to rescue troops from hostile battle zones. Like many others who were in wars, he had harrowing experiences, including a close encounter with another helicopter when he was upside down and saw the other directly above, but he never speaks about war itself. I have many friends who have experienced the unexpected topsy-turvy periods of life that resulted during mandatory conscription. I am glad those currently in the armed services have chosen to be there, and we should honor them for doing so.

I like to muse over the irony that I spent my first forty years trying to stay out of Vietnam and second forty years trying to get there. I succeeded in both.

You've Come a Long Way

Women march to demand equality, August 26, 1970.

Library of Congress, public domain, via Wikimedia Commons:
https://commons.wikimedia.org/wiki/File:Women%27s_march.jpg

Accessed August 24, 2025

The Rebel

Cecil Huey

My college years passed in the era when phone calls from home were usually a signal that something serious was afoot. Long-distance calls were rarely for chit-chat. Beside their expense, the practical impediment of single phone booths on long dormitory halls required a willing passerby to answer and then summon the intended recipient. Rings were rarely ignored completely, though, because their potential importance was understood.

So, with a little apprehension, I stepped into the phone booth one evening in 1965 for a call from home. It was my mother calling to caution me against being upset by things I might have read in the newspaper about her. I suspect, on that particular subject, calls are still rare, even in the age of cell phones.

My mother was a teacher and a patient woman, up to a point, and now she had become a rebel. She was leading a campaign in Anderson, SC, to remedy the unequal pay of men and women teachers having equal qualifications, which had not gone unnoticed. Cumbersome long-distance calls were just one regional relic of past times.

I regret not knowing the whole story, but I was away most of the time back then, and, besides, my family didn't speak of causes and ambitions and such things. My kin were all resolute and principled, sometimes to the point of stubbornness, and felt little need to discuss things that ought to be just understood.

From disconnected memories and vaguely recalled comments, I know that my mother had to weather the inchoate, Old South response to so many things in the days when *Brown v. Board of Education* was still fresh. I know she was hurt by suggestions that she was "some kind of communist or something," and by those who stopped speaking to her. But she was warmed enough by a football coach's comment, to repeat it. "This will cost me money, but it's the right thing," he said.

She kept a supporting letter signed by the faculty of one elementary school in a little cedar box along with a few other mementos. We have a large, silver compote dish engraved with the following:

> # SARA T. HUEY
> GIVEN BY THE WOMEN TEACHERS
> OF ANDERSON SCHOOL DISTRICT FIVE
> FOR HEADING THE DRIVE TO EQUALIZE
> THE SALARIES OF MEN AND WOMEN
> WITH THE SAME EXPERIENCE
> AND QUALIFICATION
> 1967

"Can't You Control Her?"

Jim Palmer

We married in 1970, the same year I was hired by the Clemson University Department of Agronomy and Soils. I met Kate Salley on a blind date at her friend's house at a party for Mexican exchange students. Since Kate's friend was a Spanish professor, the language at the party was all Spanish. Kate and I were the only two there speaking English. I should have known we were due to embrace controversy since she was formerly the cartoonist at USC's *The Gamecock* during the tumultuous sixties. Post marriage, Kate had a short-lived career as a schoolteacher but wanted to have a job where she could use her art.

With cartoons all over our house, Kate contacted a friend, the editor of our local newspaper, about freelancing with her editorial cartoons. Happily, she agreed to do editorial cartoons for $4 per cartoon. After our second child, Salley, was born, the Watergate hearings affixed Kate's attention to our television while I traveled the state working with soybean farmers.

In 1974, I drove Kate and our small children to *The Greenville News* where I said, as she exited our car, "Don't leave until somebody looks at your cartoons." With a couple of years of her commentary becoming more popular with readers, the *News* hired her as South Carolina's first full-time newspaper staff editorial cartoonist. The editor there offered her five dollars per cartoon, and she accepted.

Of course, the mid-Seventies were volatile years for politics—and for Clemson Football. Kate did a cartoon illustrating how the Clemson Board of Trustees apparently instructed the university administration to fire then head coach Red Parker. The cartoon was not well received in some quarters. As an elected member of the Faculty Senate, I later attended a holiday reception for the Board where I was introduced to a member who angrily declared that he didn't care who I was or was married to, but that he hated Kate's cartoons. "Can't you control her?" he asked. Further, a cartoon about the Clemson administration prompted another Board member to inquire about me, since I was on the faculty, "Is there nothing that can be done about him?" Thank goodness for tenure!

As Kate's career at *The Greenville News* progressed with national syndication, she joined the American Association of Editorial Cartoonists (AAEC) where she was one of only two female editorial cartoonists in North America. Although welcomed by other cartoonists, at the convention's business meeting, Kate was refused entry because she was a woman. The word she got was, "You are supposed to be down the hall at the Ladies Auxiliary meeting." Kate replied, "That's where my husband is." At another AAEC meeting in Washington, White House staff tried to deny Kate and another female cartoonist entry to the Rose Garden to hear President Reagan speak. She was told that "no ladies are allowed, only cartoonists." Kate told the person in charge, "I am not a lady! I am a cartoonist!"

Limited Opportunity

Rosanne Pruitt

As a student athlete in high school, I was set. I had just made the varsity basketball team and secured a spot on the drill team that performed at halftime of the football games. The drill team was a precision majorette-like group but without batons. I had just gotten my uniforms for both teams when I learned my dad had accepted the call to leave Georgia for a ministry position in South Carolina.

To my surprise, there were no teams for girls at my new high school. Girls could play in the band or cheer. That was it. Cheerleaders were elected by the student body, essentially a popularity contest. I tried out and was glad they did not publicize the vote since I did not yet know very many students. I was told by several that I was "too tall." Determined to play basketball, I joined a team at the local YMCA. Our team won the state championship my junior year, but we missed the recognition associated with representing our high school.

In college in the early Seventies, I contemplated medical school but once again saw the glass ceiling for women. Medical schools had only a few spots for women. It was a battle I knew I did not need to fight once I talked with the recruiter for Emory Nursing. I was told I could do everything I wanted to do and have a job option anywhere in the world once I graduated with a BS in Nursing.

Title IX of the Education Amendments became law in 1972 prohibiting sex-based discrimination at any school receiving federal funding. My former graduate school, the University of Maryland, was at the center of the battle over discrimination against females regarding pay, rank, and admission. The biggest impact of Title IX has been felt in high school and college athletics.

Title IX opened so many doors and spotlighted the discrimination against women. I have heard men grumble about the requirement for a new women's team at Clemson when a new men's team is proposed. You will find me cheering on all women's sports and all the options currently available for female athletes.

A Slow Evolution

Victoria Ridgeway Gillis

I grew up in the Forties and Fifties in a small Southern town eighteen miles east of and a hundred years behind Atlanta. There were strict dress codes back then. I wore dresses or skirts and blouses to school. No one in their right mind would have worn pants, termed "slacks" at the time. If we went to Atlanta, we wore gloves and a hat. Always. My mother had a lovely collection of gloves: summer gloves, gloves with satin lining, gloves everywhere. My daughters used to play dress-up with them . . . but I digress.

When I went off to college, we were not allowed to wear pants, unless it had snowed or there was ice on the ground. We might slip and fall and show our underwear! So, if weather permitted, it was announced that we could wear pants (NOT jeans) on selective days. I was not allowed to have a pair of jeans in my possession in college. Amazingly, it did not seem odd at the time—it just seemed normal.

In the Sixties women could not have a bank account on their own; they had to have a male co-signer on the account. I was married, and my husband's name was, therefore, required to be on my account. When we first married, we lived in Athens, Georgia, and I taught junior high science to put him through veterinary medical school. We lived on $300 per month, and I had to budget carefully to pay rent, utilities, gas for transportation, and groceries. I budgeted ten dollars per week for groceries and added up the total as I shopped each week. When I reached my limit, I put items back on the shelf.

As a newly married woman in 1968, I was horrified to discover that my husband had no idea about money. He thought that if you had checks in your checkbook, you had money in the bank. Perhaps it was not fair to expect him to think otherwise. As a college student, when he wrote a check that might bounce, the bank president in their small west Georgia town would call his father, who would instruct the bank president to put another fifty dollars in the bank for his son. Problem solved. Except now I was married to that problem.

One Saturday afternoon after I had done the laundry at the local laundromat, shopped for groceries, and cleaned house, he came in from a day of fishing so excited about his purchase of an electric boat motor. "It was on sale!" he declared.

"Why in the world did you buy a motor? We don't have a boat!" I shouted at him.

"I'm tired of paddling when Eddie and I go fishing. It was on sale—half price!"

"How much?"

After exchanging the same sentences several times, "How much," was always met with "It was on sale"—he finally admitted the electric motor had cost $100.

"Where did you get the money?" I asked.

"I wrote a check," he replied.

I said, "Mike, we don't have $100 in the account right now, I don't get paid until next week."

His response was, "But I had a check."

That moment was when I discovered his theory about bank accounts. We ate sparingly for the remainder of the month and used some of our meager savings to cover the check he had written. Unlike my husband, I had always had to watch my pennies—there was no one who could or would replenish my bank account if I ran low. At the time, though, women couldn't be trusted to have bank accounts on their own.

In the mid-Seventies, I saved money from my teaching salary to buy a house. I desperately wanted to have a home of my own and begin a family, though as I write this I am wondering about my sanity at the time. This man-child had no idea about money; how could he ever be a parent? Anyway, I saved my money and was able to put a downpayment on an 1,800-square-foot home in a new development north of Orlando, named Wekiva. But I couldn't purchase the home on my own. No, I had to have a man's name on the deed as well. Women could not be trusted with a home loan.

When credit cards came out, I could not have a credit card in my name. My credit card was in my husband's name. I was Mrs. Irresponsible-So-and-So. At the time, given the tenor of attitudes about women, it didn't seem odd or even unjust to me. But in 1980, I divorced. Suddenly, having a credit card in my name and a bank account of my own was imperative. It was also a novelty in the financial world.

The divorce catapulted me, suddenly a single mother with two small children under the age of five, into therapy. Through that process, I discovered I was a person in my own right, apart from any man.

It is a struggle to maintain "one's self," especially if you were raised to always make others happy, to never be angry (or at least never show it), to put everyone else first. Thirty-five years after that unhappy message, it took lots of therapy and volumes of personal journals to undo the damage. To this day, it is hard for me to know when I am angry—I usually discover that feeling when the anger flows out of my pen as I write in my journal. The "undoing" is never permanent. It is often too easy to slip back into "my place."

Over the years, I have gone through cycles of losing myself, then finding me again. It is a constant struggle, but one that is worth it. After nearly 80 years on this earth, I have finally reached the age of selfhood—I don't care what others think, I am going to be me. If they don't like it, that's fine. I do.

Evolving Rights of Women

Dolores (Dee) Stegelin

My perspective. Sometimes in life our experiences form a pattern that we don't fully understand or appreciate while we are undergoing them. Such was the case for me as a teenager maturing into a young woman during the Sixties. In time, I realized growing up as the oldest daughter on a dairy farm positioned me for much responsibility at an early age. I loved the outdoors, all the animals, and the excitement of the daily rhythm of activities on the farm: feeding calves and lambs; cuddling the warm, fluffy Border Collie puppies; and feeling that I was an integral part of the farm itself. In that role, I gladly accepted my father's directions and assigned chores, and these early experiences strengthened my sense of self and confidence.

My formative life experiences as a female in rural Kansas were also influenced greatly by my parents' religious beliefs. My father's side of the family originated with the Amish and Mennonite immigrants who came to the United States from Germany and Switzerland in the 1700s. My paternal grandparents were born in Kansas to Mennonites who had traveled to Kansas from their original roots in Lancaster, Pennsylvania, where many Mennonite families landed in the 1700s. Rooted in these conservative beliefs were certain expectations of women, who were to assume a supportive role to their husbands. These women were strong individuals, both physically and mentally. They often helped their husbands with farmwork and then assumed nearly all the responsibilities for cooking, cleaning, and running the household. However, men were the decision-makers and breadwinners.

My father, however, did not expect my mother to milk the cows or drive the tractor. He felt that women should not be burdened with all those roles, and my mother enjoyed a domestic life and was in charge of the household. They found a balance in which they were both happy.

Along with these assumptions about gender roles, girls were also not to witness certain activities on the farm, such as watching a cow or ewe give birth to their calves and lambs. I was sent to the house when these "sensitive" activities were taking place. Yet I felt cheated because my older brother was privy to these activities, and he would tease me because I wasn't allowed to do everything that he was. These were my first experiences as a female coming to realize we were not equal to our male counterparts.

Assisting the vet, an eye opener. One day my father called our family veterinarian to come out and assist a cow that was really struggling with the birth of her calf. It was a very busy time, and my father and older brother were very engaged in all the tasks associated with the wheat harvest. So, my father directed me to tell the vet where the cow was located so he could go and assist her. Much to my surprise (and delight), the vet drove into our driveway and waved for me to come to the car. I went to his car and pointed to where the cow was situated in our large pasture. He said to me, "Hop in and ride with me—I'm probably going to need some help with this." I was shocked—what would Daddy think?

I opened the passenger door and crawled into the front seat with the vet. We drove out to the pasture and located the cow, which, by now, was exhausted and very wary of the vet's arrival. He gave me my assignment: sit by the cow's head, hold it down, and comfort her while he helped deliver the calf. I felt VERY important as I knelt by the cow's head and talked to her while the vet did his work. Finally, the calf emerged and was deemed to be healthy. The cow, weak and relieved, quickly turned her attention to her new calf. The vet gathered up his equipment, loaded his car, and directed me to get into the car so he would take me back to the house. You can only imagine how excited I was to tell my father and brother all about this exciting experience! That was one small step in gaining my status on the farm, even though I was a girl.

Strong Mennonite women. Lest I leave the impression that Mennonite women were somehow timid or weak, I wish very much to clarify. In fact, looking back at my childhood, I see that I was surrounded by many very strong females. My father's mother—a tiny woman in physical stature—had helped with all the work on the farm as well as all the responsibilities in the house and with the children. My grandmother was a master gardener as well as an excellent cook. She possessed the classic Pennsylvania Dutch work ethic along with creativity and resourcefulness. Grandma could make the best meals from leftovers! For many years she milked cows, harvested crops, and then went to the house to do all the chores there. I have fond memories of extended family picnics on Sunday afternoons with many of my female adult relatives wearing long dark dresses and bonnets. They were warm and caring people.

Aunt Adda, another strong woman of the Sixties. Among my favorite older relatives was great Aunt Adda, sister to my paternal grandmother and aunt to my father. She was sometimes called "the Old Maid," which I found cruel. She had been engaged to marry but her fiancé was killed in an accident, so she chose never to marry. She was my favorite older female relative. Even then I knew she was stronger than most other women. She had suffered the loss of her fiancé, yet she went on to get formal training as a nurse. She was fun and funny, and she loved being around her nieces and nephews. Like her sister, my grandmother, Aunt Adda was a tiny but energetic woman. She was strong, feisty, and an important part of the fabric of my extended family.

Among the many rich memories I have as an undergraduate student at Kansas State, one really stands out: a visit from Aunt Adda. As a freshman I was assigned to a dorm room on the top floor of a dorm—a penthouse suite! My room was right across the hallway from the vending machine area, and that's where I came to love Dr. Pepper. It was a bustling, always busy place with a large commons area surrounded by hallways leading to rooms each shared by two female freshman students. In those days, we had a 10:00 pm curfew and bed check, and it became my "home" during my first year in college. In retrospect, female college students in the Sixties had many restrictions when compared with female students in 2025!

Aunt Adda was not five feet tall, even with her Mennonite bonnet! She had a magical personality and sense of humor, and she was fascinated with my decision to go to Kansas State. She told me that she wanted to see what my life was like as a freshman at this "huge" university. I didn't know when she was coming, only that she planned to come "sometime." So, one Sunday afternoon, she drove by herself the fifty miles from Abilene to Manhattan, KS, to pay a visit to me at my dorm on the sixth floor of Moore Hall at Kansas State University.

On this particular Sunday afternoon, I received a call from the first floor resident assistant that I had a visitor who had been cleared and to expect her soon. With that limited information, I awaited my guest. Imagine my surprise when off the elevator came Aunt Adda—all 4'10" of her in her Mennonite dress and bonnet. The girls in the dorm were enchanted by her. We offered her some Dr. Pepper from the vending machine, showed her our rooms, and hosted her in my room for conversation and lots of good stories and laughter.

I was so taken by Aunt Adda's visit that I wrote about the experience in my English Composition class and got an A on that paper! To this day, Aunt Adda's surprise visit, in her Mennonite garb and jolly, humorous personality, remains one of my favorite college memories.

Becoming an officer's wife. It was February 1970, and I was fresh out of college and just 23 when I married. My husband had just graduated with a degree in agriculture, and he had a five-year Air Force ROTC commitment to complete. I had no experience related to the military life, so I had a steep learning curve when I became an Air Force officer's wife. I quickly learned that wives had their place: support your husband, follow the directives of the military, and ask no questions. Yet I was a naturally curious person, and I was used to asking questions. So, when my husband was going through training to be a navigator, and when he was ordered overseas for a year's deployment on very short notice, I had questions. I asked the base commander so many questions, he finally told me that if anything happened to my husband, I would be the first to know as he would personally call me and give me information. Well, that worked. And I trusted him!

You can imagine my shock when my husband's plane was shot down, and I learned about it from a call directly from my husband when he was recovering in a military "MASH" hospital in Udorn, Thailand! I ended up calling the base commander and informing him what had happened! With time and perspective, I realized that war is unpredictable and that the commander did not know about the incident at first. Communication channels during wartime are complex and not dependable.

As late as 1970 I was not able to have a credit card on my own. My husband had to have the credit card, and I could use it with his permission. So, it is safe to say that over my seven plus decades of living, the roles of women have evolved immensely. I do think the Sixties and Seventies introduced a revolution in thinking about women's rights, but the changes in our culture have been slow to come. I give credit to my strong Mennonite female ancestors for being such good role models. They inspired me to be my best and to stretch my dreams as far as I could. Thank you, Aunt Adda, and thanks to all the other strong women who influenced me in my formative years, including the many female faculty members at Kansas State University—you opened a whole new world to me.

Toward Life Choices

Debra Broadwell Jackson

I graduated in May 1971 from the Medical University of South Carolina with a baccalaureate degree in nursing. In early summer we met in Columbia, S C. and sat for the written license examinations for nurses. The test was divided into five books: medical, surgical, pediatric, obstetrics, and psychiatric. You could pass one or all the segments. If you failed one segment, you could retake it. We waited for weeks for our scores. In 2025, the test is given on a computer. You know your score before you leave the room. In 1971, we had no study guides or courses for preparing for the exam. We arrived in Columbia, with our notes and textbooks, having been reviewing for weeks. I kept those textbooks for years and had most of my handwritten notes as well. They were discarded when I moved to Clemson in 1990!

I worked that summer of '71 in Charleston, saving every penny for my move to Atlanta. My roommates called the nurses' station one afternoon and asked me if I wanted them to open the letter from the South Carolina Board of Nursing and tell me if I had passed. I told them to open the envelope. I was relieved to learn I had passed, and my scores were good for licensure in South Carolina and Georgia. With test scores in hand, I quickly applied for a

Georgia license. I would begin my adult life and would learn several important lessons along the way.

Don't make decisions for others, particularly women.
I was assigned to a renal medical unit which was led by Billie (my female head nurse) who organized the nurses into two teams. Two new graduates arrived that month. Each team received one newbie. The team was not thrilled to have someone new to train but was grateful for a warm body to help out. My teammates had extremely high standards and expectations. All patients were referred to the hospital, usually from other physicians and hospitals. The patients on the unit had unusual conditions. Their diagnoses ranged from infectious diseases to renal failure. It was not unusual for families to be absent; most patients did not live in the greater Atlanta area.

Fifty years ago, the technology we see today did not exist. If a patient needed 100 cc of intravenous fluid over eight hours, you had to count each drop and compute how many drops per minute were needed. The pharmacy did not bring the medications in nice, neat containers for a single patient. The hardest part of a medical unit is the number and timing of medications required. Calculating drug dosages and knowing any side effects or contraindications and patient allergies are required.

Our unit provided peritoneal dialysis on the unit for patients in renal failure. Hemodialysis machines were used as well, and a technician sat by the bedside during the process to ensure that the blood flow through the machine was managed properly and the tubing did not separate from the shunts entering the blood vessels. During my first year, the first renal transplant at Emory Hospital was performed. The recipient came back to our floor and my team for care. The primary surgeon selected the three nurses he trusted the most to care for the patient. I was not one of the three but provided support to those who were in full isolation to protect the patient and unable to leave the room.

One of the most interesting cases involved a young man whose skin was orange. He had extensive diagnostic tests done. One of the interns on the unit noticed during the admission interview that the young man drank a great deal of carrot juice. He proposed blood work for beta-carotene levels which turned out to be extremely high. This was the correct diagnosis. The intern's reputation was enhanced significantly.

We also had a young woman admitted to the unit who had been exposed to an unusual respiratory infection. She worked in a medical laboratory and ran the tests on a male patient sample and was infected during the process of analyzing the sample. She was a new mom. The original male patient had also been transferred to our unit from the same small Georgia hospital. The intravenous medication they were given had to be handled carefully and the bottle of fluid and tubing wrapped to prevent exposure to light. The male patient lived. The new mom died. I still remember her husband bringing her baby in for a visit before she died. It was so sad and an experience I would see again.

A second 20-year-old woman was admitted without a definitive diagnosis. She was short, thin, and had dark hair and eyes. When I talked with her, she showed me pictures of her husband and baby. The baby appeared to be in a bassinet. As we talked, I learned that her husband and baby had recently died in a car crash. I looked again at the baby's picture. It was not in a bassinet; it was in a coffin. It was the only picture of her baby she had. She spent several weeks on the unit before she died. I often wondered if she had willed herself to join her family. I do not remember any family visiting her during the weeks she was on the unit. Later I would learn pictures of deceased family members in coffins were common and would take pictures for families at their request.

One afternoon, at the end of the shift, I admitted a man who had a "bad" cough, according to the referral hospital and ambulance personnel. No one was in isolation gear, so the EMT helped us to get him into a bed. We decided to request isolation protocols. I was responsible for obtaining sputum specimens for analysis. As I held a cup for the man to spit in, he turned his head and intentionally spit into my hand. I was so angry and appalled by his behavior. He never knew how close I came to wiping his spit in his face. Instead, I wiped it into the cup and sent it to the lab. Washing my hands in the hottest water and betadine soap I could tolerate, I left for the day. I do not mind pee and poop. I will hold a pan for someone to vomit (notice I said pan, because I will gag with them). But sputum is gross.

The man's test came back: tuberculosis. As a result, we were all required to have a tuberculin skin test done. Of the entire staff, I was the only person who tested positive. I spent the next year taking isoniazid, having lung x-rays, and getting blood work for abnormal liver enzymes. For years, my tuberculin skin tests (required annually at that time for hospital workers) remained positive, and I was required to have x-rays of my lungs. Workman's comp followed me closely and did cover the expenses.

Billie decided I needed something positive and challenging. We had a 45-year-old gentleman, Sam, who was admitted with diabetes, and he needed to learn how to live and cope with the disease. Billie wanted me to develop a patient education plan for diabetes, work with the nutritionist, and teach Sam to test his blood, calculate his insulin dose, and inject his insulin. I was thrilled at the opportunity. I worked on a teaching plan. He would be hospitalized for one week. For the next five days, I spent hours with Sam and his wife. He was doing great. I left on Friday afternoon and he was scheduled for discharge Saturday morning.

A month later, while taking the report for my night rotation, the nurse doing the report, a part-time team member, said, "It was really sad about Sam, wasn't it?" I asked what she meant. She realized she had made a mistake. It seems Sam had a massive heart attack the Saturday morning he was scheduled for discharge and died. The entire unit had decided not to tell me. They wanted to protect me. While I appreciated their caring, I was furious with their assumption that I could not handle Sam's death.

I still get angry when someone thinks they should protect me by hiding something that might be upsetting. What is more upsetting than having two young moms die or being the primary nurse during a CPR that results in a death?

Women are stronger than we appear. We can manage complex environments, complex jobs, and make good decisions. We may want partners and team members, but we don't need to be protected.

Promotions may be dangerous territory. In January 1973, Billie once again approached me. It was time for my first evaluation, and she said I was doing well. In fact, Billie was recommending me for a promotion to a management position. She had met with the Associate Director of Nursing, and new plans were being developed to expand the hospital. The new wing would have seven floors, and each floor would consist of two regular units and an intensive care unit. The two head nurses would be called nurse clinicians, hold baccalaureate degrees, and a clinical nurse specialist with a master's degree would oversee the three units.

In the plans, the renal/medical unit and the urology unit would occupy a floor which contained an intensive care unit focused on dialysis and renal failure. Because I had eighteen months in renal/medicine and there was an open head nurse position in Urology, the nursing administrator recommended me. I interviewed with the director of nursing, the clinical nurse specialist, and the chief of urology. I started two weeks later.

I met my new staff and was surprised by their coolness. I realized they had no idea that I was appointed to the position. Their current nursing leader was on maternity leave. The staff felt that she was relieved of her duties and not by choice. They were angry. To add to their grievances, they were not provided an opportunity to apply for the position. It took many months before I felt a level of acceptance by the staff on the unit.

The salary was better; the hours appeared better but were not. I now had to "train" new staff members, evaluate staff, and ensure that doctors, patients, and family members were happy. I knew I needed more information and education to be an effective leader.

In March, a notice was posted at the nursing station by the School of Nursing. It seemed that the federal government had cut nursing training funds for 1973. Education at Emory was expensive and all master's students were full-time, supported by training grants to cover tuition and living expenses. The school was concerned about a significant drop in enrollment and being quick to respond to crises; they immediately implemented a part-time program of study. The school provided two avenues: two years of study or three. I applied and was admitted into the two-year program. The university's employee assistance program would cover up to five credit hours each term for employees who had been at Emory for one year. I applied for the tuition assistance and paid the difference for any hours above five. I worked full time and went to school part-time.

In August 1974, my friend, Suzanne, approached me and told me about an open position. The director of a non-degree nursing program located in the Department of Surgery was open. The program was funded by a National Cancer Institute training grant. The current position holder was a nursing faculty member. There were no application forms to complete; I just told Suzanne I would be interested. Within a week, I had interviews with the hospital's Director of Nursing and the Chief of Surgery. I was offered the position. I was thrilled. I told my thesis advisor. The next morning, I received a phone call from the Dean of Nursing. She was not thrilled. I do not think my thesis advisor was happy either. The dean made sure I realized that the job did not include a faculty appointment, and she hoped it would not affect my continued graduate course work. (It would be 1983 before I would be hired by this dean as an Associate Professor of Nursing.). I learned to never burn bridges; you might be able to use them later.

I graduated in 1975 from Emory University. On May 12th, 2025, I was inducted into the Society of Corpus Cordis Aureum (the Golden Corps of the Heart). Fifty years later, the university provided an opportunity to join the graduation procession on the Emory Quadrangle. I had nineteen years at Emory, as a staff nurse, nurse clinician, director of a non-degree nursing program, and finally a tenured associate professor of nursing. I had attended graduations throughout those years as a faculty member on the first Monday of May. I never considered that in fifty years I would have an opportunity to return.

Graduate school, research, and values. My first semester in graduate school consisted of two courses. One was graduate research. The faculty member was in the process of a research study and asked the class of seventy to participate. We could decline, but it did not seem like a good idea in your first semester to not help your faculty member with her research.

She discussed her work in the terms of feminism. A basic question she asked was how traditional or nontraditional were nurses. In the culture of the *Roe v. Wade* decision, marches for women's rights and equal pay, and many other issues, it seemed that the questions might relate to nurses in their workplaces. Nurses were employed in hospitals, doctor's offices, public health agencies, public schools, the military, and industries. It was well documented in the literature that nurses changed positions and locations regularly. Whether it was the hours required, family obligations, work conditions, or simply salary and bonuses that drove the change was the question.

Within several weeks, the faculty member returned with the results, which she described in detail. She handed us our "scores." She provided the range from the most traditional to the most nontraditional member of the class. My best friend, KC, was the most nontraditional, and I was the most traditional. It made no sense. If you examined our lifestyles, I was the most nontraditional. I was self-supporting, independent, lived in downtown Atlanta (not the suburbs), was purchasing my own home (with no male co-signature), and in an administrative position. I should not have to mention the fact that it was difficult for a single woman to buy a house without a male co-signer. The mortgage company was concerned and mentioned the issue to me. In fact, his comment came with an unwelcome proposal of how he might help. As I turned down his offer of help, I realized that the loan application could fail.

KC and I laughed for hours about the results of the survey and tried to analyze the questions to figure out how they were coded into categories and how accurate and valid the study was. We discussed at length the rights of women in the workplace, in the home, and the discrimination we had experienced in the male-dominated healthcare environment. While most nurses were women, most administrators and most doctors were men, and they were in control.

What did it truly mean to be a feminist? According to *Britannica*, "feminism is the belief in full social, economic, and political equality for women." Okay. I agreed with the feminist definition in 1973 and still do in 2025. My faculty member implied in her research discussion that a person who valued traditions, or perhaps traditional roles for women within society, could not also be a feminist. I thought the purpose of the women's movement was that women could do both, have a meaningful career and have a family. That a woman could do anything she wanted. I have.

I agree that in the Sixties, and even in the Seventies, women had fewer choices in careers. Nursing and teaching were two of the most common careers, but certainly women had other alternatives as well. Perhaps the issue goes back to the guidance counselors who guided young women without providing them broader perspectives. I am not sure that the questionnaire used was valid or that nontraditional equaled feminist was correct. Were the questions biased in one direction? Should a positive or negative connotation to either traditional or nontraditional roles of women be assigned? Can a person not be both? Can one value a traditional role in the family, while continuing a nontraditional approach in the workplace. I have had a wonderful career and a wonderful family. You can have both. It just takes work.

Abortion

Kenneth Steven Marsh

Like most of us, I entered college right out of high school at age eighteen. It was the first time I had a chance to be on my own except for two days en route to visit my uncle and family in Geneva, Switzerland, in 1963. I worked at a combination gas station and British automobile sales place to save money to extend the Switzerland trip such that I could spend two days in London. In retrospect, I could say that I might've been intelligent, but boy was I naïve when I arrived at college.

I had not dated much in high school. I wasn't really a geek, but it just didn't happen. I did go to a prom, but I didn't have a date and did not have a single dance. I was on stage with five other members of The Six Notes, supplying the music for the prom. As you might expect, when a young male is on his own in a new college setting with lots of young females, obviously, things happen.

Well, some lovely and unexpected things did happen. I met a wonderful girl—or was it a woman? At that age in life, it seems that neither word quite accurately applies. She pulled me out of my shell further than I had ventured previously, and I found myself with a pregnant girlfriend. I was willing to get married, but that really was not a great option for either of us. We explored abortion, but in 1966, abortion wasn't legal.

The truth of the matter is that abortion was and always has been available. If you have the money, there is no barrier. The issue is not whether abortions are available. The issue is whether safe abortions are available. With some searching and help from family and friends and professionals, we were able to accomplish our task safely, and a few years later I did propose to that same woman. It didn't work out, but the future was our decision, not one forced upon us by our youthful and naïve indiscretion.

In 1973, the *Roe v. Wade* decision came from the U.S. Supreme Court and made abortion legal in the United States. This meant that anyone could get a safe abortion not just those of means.

Abortion is a very personal and very difficult decision. It belongs with the people involved, their doctors and family members as appropriate. It really is nobody else's business unless the couple wants it to be. There is no politician that knows more about the situation than the couple involved.

The *Roe v. Dobbs* decision brings everything up for discussion again. The guideline for abortion in the past has basically been the viability of the fetus. Now the argument is based on when a human life begins. Claiming that life begins at inception is naïve in that every fertilized human egg does not grow to term nor should it. The human body can detect imbalances and act accordingly if the fetus is nonviable. We might not agree with that natural selection, but we have no choice in the matter.

The arguments are based on religious principles that attempt to define when life begins. Is it upon conception? At a heartbeat? Upon viability? After college? It would seem valid to the people making those arguments, but the establishment clause of the U.S. Constitution says that religion should not be imposed upon others (we cannot establish a state religion). Therefore, we can have differences of opinion based on religion, but those should never be coded into law.

From a legal standpoint, life has always begun at birth. No other point is identifiable. Drinking, driving, voting, ability to buy certain items are based upon one's age since birth. No other measure makes sense in our society.

Both my former girlfriend and I were enriched by the experiences in our lives and were able to proceed towards becoming productive citizens rather than a couple that would've been severely handicapped if burdened with a child at an age before we were ready. Now decades later I can see how things worked out with two married sons and three grandsons that are an amazing joy. Things worked out well. So, abortion should not be a legal issue nor a religious issue, but rather a health and societal issue.

Women's Rights in Colombia and the U.S.

Clementina E. Adams

My experience on the matter of women's rights comes from my experience as a citizen of both Colombia and the United States. In Colombia, I remembered how the word "mother" meant "housewife" because that was expected by society. Men were the sustainers and the ones to pursue university degrees. That situation continued until the beginning of my college years in the Sixties.

Over the years, there have been many attempts to deal with the unfair situations faced by women. Because of the tradition of male supremacy, there were many cases of sexual abuse, even in the Sixties, but too often with no clear punishment for the aggressor. In Colombia, women's rights have seen significant advancements based on amendments to our constitution. Some of the reforms guarantee the right to bodily integrity, voting, and equal access to education and employment. However, despite the progress on legal protection, there are persisting disparities, particularly in political representation and the impact of gender-based violence.

During the civil war in Colombia and the beginnings of the National Front movement (1958-1969), women's political activism was largely overshadowed by the political dynamics between the two dominant political parties. During that armed conflict in Colombia during the Sixties, women's roles were important. Women served as nurses, spies, and some even fought on the battlefields, often disguised as men. They even took on the responsibility of doing essential tasks usually done by men, such as managing farms and businesses, while their owners and workers were fighting in the Colombian civil war. Women were pivotal in organizing groups to raise funds for the war effort.

Initially, all of the Colombian schools were separated by gender. During my elementary and high school years, I was always surrounded by girls as classmates and women as teachers. In my first year of college, I was amazed to see males in our classes as well as male professors. We were so accustomed to the separation of boys and girls in school that, initially at recess times, we formed our separate groups of friends based on gender. Eventually, we began to interact with our male classmates through assigned teamwork activities.

During the Sixties I began to notice the increase in the number of women entering into the world of academics. We also had our first women as professors, mainly brought from England and the U.S. At the end of the Sixties more Colombian women professors started to be part of the university's faculty. This change also occurred in the health market professions as they became more open to women, not only as nurses, but as medical doctors.

Once, when I was a child starting elementary school, I was playing with one of my friends in her house. Suddenly, I heard crying and a lament coming from one of the bedrooms. I went in to investigate and I saw my friend's older sister crying while looking at her baby as he slept in his crib. I asked her why she was crying, and she hugged me and said that her husband was not a good person. I saw purple and red spots on her body. I asked her who punished her, and she replied that it was her husband. Immediately, I asked, why don't you leave him and live with your own family. She smiled and told me to go back to play and not to worry. After a couple of years, my friend told me that her sister had finally left her abusive husband. A bold act at that time.

Even as a young girl, I realized that women had to deal with bad men that mistreated them. In my high school years, we saw posters advocating for better treatment of women and for allowing more participation in political parties and governmental jobs. I also saw women on television promoting the need for equal participation in all areas of businesses and especially in leadership roles in their respective regions of the country. Similar televised programs on those issues appeared in the U.S. broadcast systems. In the Sixties I observed how excited my female relatives and my mother were about casting their ballots during elections. Then, I was surprised to learn that women had only gained the right to vote in 1954.

In college, we discussed the unfairness of the small number of women involved in political representation. Another pressing topic was women's right to equal opportunity employment. In fact, when I began working in Colombia after college, I was fortunate to have the same job opportunity and salary level as any man who applied for the same job. However, there are still some gaps that need to be closed. This situation is similar in the U.S.

Currently, Colombia has ratified all current international treaties related to women's rights. Colombian women have enjoyed deserved victories related to gender equality in employment, promotion, and societal areas of life. There is continual work on enacting laws to promote gender equality. Among those efforts are the Public

Policy Guidelines for Women's Gender Equality, and the Comprehensive Plan to ensure that women can live free of violence.

However, I can sadly conclude that even after many amendments to the constitutions and efforts by representatives from both Colombia and the U.S., there is still much to do to finally close the gender gap for equality of treatment and protection. In addition, we must continue to create permanent and equal employment opportunities for women. Protection from violence and sexual abuse and appropriate punishment for abusers remains a critical issue.

Reflections

Composition Book

Name: _____

Subject: _____

Date: _____

Senior Press
29670

Harvey Gantt, Clemson University's first Black student
speaks with reporters.
January 28, 1963

Clemson University Digital Collections

https://digitalcollections.clemson.edu/wp-content/uploads/2016/11/Harvey_Gantt_
being_interviewed.jpg

Accessed September 23, 2025

Reverse:

Artwork by Cecil Huey

Blowin' in the Wind

Marty Duckenfield

As I look back, I recognize that the Sixties were turbulent times for America, yet early in those years, with the exception of the Kennedy assassination, little turbulence found its way to my doorstep, whether in my early life as a youngster in a village not far from New York City, later amid the snows blanketing a college campus in New England, or yet later on the far-off shores of Britain. Without the benefit of television for most of that time, I blissfully went through the years tuned in to my personal world and was only vaguely aware of the Sixties as a backdrop: the twin traumas of the Vietnam War and the Civil Rights Movement.

I went to a small college in Maine, and in my junior year, 1965-66, I became an adventurer by going to England to study British history. Life in the U.S. seemed so far away, although I recall being embarrassed by newspaper images of LBJ crassly showing the world his abdominal surgical scars after gall bladder surgery. His conduct did not improve his image in the less exhibitionist culture of Great Britain any more favorably than his previously photographed practice of lifting his beagles by the ears had impressed this dog-loving country. Other than that, not much news filtered in, especially when, besides the daily diversions of living there, opportunities to see TV news was a rarity, and when seen, the focus was on England.

Consequently, when I returned to the States, it was to a different country although certainly recognizable after only a year. Back in Maine, my senior year of 1966-1967 found my male classmates and some of my dormmates' boyfriends suddenly facing their futures with greater concern as the draft was busy inducting young men. Would they sign up or get drafted? Would they go to graduate school or get married? All these options related to Vietnam, which touched me only tangentially, and although interested and concerned about my classmates, we had our senior year and finals to deal with. And I had Chris, my English boyfriend who was at the nearby University of Connecticut, to visit on weekends, so that seemed enough for the moment.

Even so, my attention was always attuned to the music of the times. My roommate Shirley's records had been the background for our sophomore year, but when revisited in this new climate of our senior year in 1966, along with my own maturity, the folk protest songs began to resonate. Peter, Paul, and Mary were singing the anthems of our times, which touched me deeply that year, opening an emotional channel that would soon lead me to take steps to oppose the war and advocate for Civil Rights. I finally clearly heard the memorable words of Bob Dylan's "Blowin' in the Wind."

My postgraduation life found me learning to teach in Connecticut. I was teaching seventh-grade Language Arts and Social Studies in Ellington, Connecticut, a rural community east of Hartford. I was 21 years old and woefully unprepared, so I had long days trying to learn the most challenging job I had ever had. My roommate and I watched the evening news before we corrected papers, and the outside world began to seep into my consciousness. Nevertheless, I was consumed with my students and their lives, grocery shopping and cooking each night, and weekly visits to the laundromat; and of course, spending time with Chris.

In 1968, my second year of teaching, we got married, and Chris, being an international graduate student, became extremely interested in the American political process, so therefore, so did I. Early that year, we went to a rally in Hartford at the Bushnell Auditorium to hear Senator Eugene McCarthy, a senator bold enough to challenge President Johnson for the presidency. He was antiwar, and his audience consisted of many college students, so in many ways, at the young age of 22, we fit right in with the audience's demographic—who were mostly antiwar.

I had already had my heart opened to McCarthy's profound message by the words of "Blowin' in the Wind," but at the rally, my mind was finally opened as well. Along with the daily backdrop of the TV war images, my antiwar position was solidified by Senator McCarthy's rationale for getting out of a war that had already gone on far too long. I found that people I knew felt strongly on both sides of the issue and voiced their opinions. I mostly kept silent, though, listening closely to those who shared their thoughts, all the while becoming absorbed into a new political awareness.

We all know about the further earthshaking, traumatic events of 1968, which were unlike anything most of us, particularly from my generation, had ever experienced. How would I deal with it? I always return to the music: I had finally bought my own copy of Peter, Paul, and Mary's record, and as I navigated those tumultuous times, the music continued to ground me as I followed my heart—and my mind as well.

The South Carolina State House
The lower banner is the Confederate battle flag.

The Confederate flag was first displayed above the State House in 1961 to commemorate of the start of the Civil War. It remained there for 54 years before being removed in 2015 following the murder of nine Black parishioners of Emanuel AME Church in Charleston, SC.

The image above appeared in the official South Carolina Legislative Manual of 1963[1] leading an account of the history of the State House. It ran without change from 1963 to 1980.

Over the period of the "long decade" the Confederate flag appeared on the cover of the Legislative Manual seven times and in numerous contexts within the manual. Other images depicting the Confederate States of America appeared on the cover of the manual twice more during the time.

---

[1] General Assembly of South Carolina, Legislative Manual - General Assembly of South Carolina, Inez Watson, Ed. 1963.

The Sixties-South:
A First-Person Ramble

Cecil Huey

Sixty years ago, Bob Dylan warned us that the times were "a-changin'," but I didn't get the message. Maybe, because I was more into beach music—Maurice Williams and that sort of thing—except we didn't call it beach music. We called it music.

I was a Southern, white-boy, preppy jock, and I can't remember what I thought at the time, owing less to poor memory than to the fact that I wasn't thinking about much of anything. While there was fun to be had and schoolwork to study, little time remained for deep thinking. Just about everyone I knew shared the boat. Now, here I am today, trying to recall times past and assess my reactions to them, and, at this remove, my efforts are unavoidably informed by all that passed in the interim and, of course, the thoughts of others.

Thinking back, I find it helpful to view the Sixties as a "long decade," demarked on one end by the landmark *Brown v. Board of Education* school desegregation decision of 1954 and on the other by the end of the decade. It was punctuated throughout by historically significant happenings including the Vietnam War and the moon landing of 1969. I see the Brown decision as a "natural" starting point because of the substantial impetus it added to the tide of social change that followed. In South Carolina, it triggered shock, indignation, angst, and in some quarters, optimism and jubilation, all intensified by the recognition that its nexus was a Charleston courtroom.

A few questions emerge right off the bat: what explains our complacency in the midst of historic times, why were we so late to the game, and why are some of us yet to hear Dylan? The answers, I believe, lie in the scrambled intersection of time, place, and events, the "Sixties-South," I'll call it, and our being, at once, South Carolinians and South Carolinian—four coupled entities, "when," "where," "what," and "us." To avoid overbroad implications, I emphasize that references to "we" and "us" apply to me and my crowd, and the notions offered reflect a personal view from within that crowd and have no authority beyond that. I will focus on our response to the historical period rather than to particular events.

Dredging up old memories, thoughts, and impressions is a fraught endeavor. Doing so and trying to judge them now against a larger historical reference is inevitably personal and forces a measure of self-assessment. Preventing self-assessment from becoming self-justification requires honesty to an uncomfortable degree. It's daunting, but here goes.

I remember personally significant things. I remember the assassinations; I remember the war and learning of friends lost to it; I remember my draft notice; I remember Bull Connor's dogs; I remember "one small step for man," and I remember parties and athletic contests. I remember *Huckleberry Finn*, *The Grapes of Wrath*, *To Kill a Mockingbird*, and *Silent Spring*. I remember racial segregation, churchgoing, and optimism.

Also, I remember disgraceful things that went unremarked by most of us. I remember grade-school minstrel shows, blackface and all. I remember Confederate flags fluttering over the state capital and over football games. I remember that flag reflected on Clemson University basketball uniforms. I remember whites-only "academies" sprouting like weeds, many rooted in mainline churches, all aimed at avoiding integration. I remember Confederate Memorial Day as a state holiday, and I recall being startled by interracial couples, Black folks in previously unaccustomed roles, and Clemson's first Black athletes. The "Lost Cause" was accepted doctrine.

Clemson University's Basketball Team (1961)
(Note the Confederate flag motif reflected on the shorts.)
Source: Clemson University Taps, 1961

Such things were experienced widely and are remembered everywhere. That, for us, these things were by turn, significant, horrifying, unremarkable, or startling reflects who we were, South Carolinians and South Carolinian. In trying to sift meaning and relevance from our experience of the long decade, I have come to believe that, of the "what-when-where-us" continuum, the "us" was dominant. Accordingly, I will try to illuminate that element by briefly examining certain of its roots.

First, to get at the notion of being both South Carolinians and South Carolinian, I'll start with the Works Progress Administration (WPA) guide to South Carolina. The guide is a product of the Federal Writers Project and is very much of its time, the late 1930s. It starts with a remarkable essay, "Who is the South Carolinian?" The essay startled me when I first encountered it, and I've read it many times. Natives of the state likely take exception to parts of it, but having friends and relatives sprinkled across the entire state, I marvel at the authors' perception and at the persisting relevance of their insights when I reflect on the Sixties-South. It rewards the reading. Within it are these comments:

"One had to live in South Carolina to realize the difference that, seen from the outside, become subordinated to one or two great common attributes. South Carolinians are among the rare folk in the South who have no secret envy of Virginians. They have a love for their own State which is a phalanx against all attacks of whatever order.

[The South Carolinian] … "prefers his personal standards of right and wrong to those prescribed in courts of law, and his own opinions are much more important to him than those of legally appointed judges…

"…He knows his faults, at least many of them. He will discuss them and propose remedies—but woe to the outsider who reminds him of them…[2]"

And, in the Sixties, everyone on TV was an outsider.

Next, I cite a grade-school text[3], customarily termed the Simms History of South Carolina. It was used in a mandated state history course and now remains rich in additional insight into early twentieth century South

---

[2] South Carolina: The WPA Guide to the Palmetto State, Univ. of SC Press (Reprint), 1988.
[3] Mary C. Simms Oliphant: The History of South Carolina (1922)

Carolina. It was a staple in the state's public schools and an approved text for over sixty years.

Think about that: a single history text used widely for sixty years. It was racist, through and through, and it both reflected and sustained old attitudes across generations of South Carolinians. The influence was profound, pernicious, and lasting, and it haunts us yet. A quick browse of the full text (one click away on-line[4]) is worth the effort, especially the post-Civil War period through Reconstruction into the early 20th Century. A few snippets follow. They are at once insightful and horrifying. I believe they stand alone without comment.

PREFACE

THE purpose in revising Simms' History of South Carolina was to make the book better suited for study by grade pupils. The book has been entirely re-written and the text greatly simplified.

---

288. Condition of the Slaves. As we shall hear much a little later on about the evils of slavery, it should be said now that the slave owners in South Carolina, as a rule, treated their negroes with the greatest kindness, fed them well and clothed them comfortably. A negro slave cost money and a slave owner would no more have thought of mistreating a slave and making him unfit to work than he would have thought of abusing a fine horse. On the plantations the negroes lived in little houses near the "big house" of their masters. When they were ill they were cared for. As they were not worked too hard, they led a care free life because their masters provided for all their needs.

---

[4] Full text available at this site: https://babel.hathitrust.org/cgi/pt?id=loc.ark:/13960/t8hd84268&view=1up&seq=1)
Accessed August 20, 2025

CHAPTER XXX

OVERTHROW OF RADICAL GOVERNMENT

434. The Ku-Klux Klan. Secret organizations of white men were formed in nearly all the conquered states of the South. The men in these organizations were determined to hold the freed slaves in check and to fight the evil-doing radicals. These secret organizations were called the Ku-Klux Klan. In South Carolina, the military officers had given way to Scott and his government, but the Federal soldiers were held in the State to enforce the will of the radicals. The Ku-Klux Klan secretly decided to oppose the radicals as well as to protect the women and children of the State. The Ku-Klux met only at night. They were always mounted on horses and wore caps and masks to conceal their faces and long white coats which covered them and fell down over their horses. The sight of these ghostly riders galloping by in the night was a very terrifying one to the superstitious negro. A visit from the Ku-Klux was sufficient in most cases to turn him away from his evil doing.

469. Constitution of 1895. In 1894 the demand for a new Constitution had grown to such proportions that the legislature called for an election of delegates to form a Convention for the purpose of making a new Constitution. The Convention was held in Columbia in 1895. The most important question before the Convention was framing new election laws. This was necessary so as to give the white people protection against an overwhelming and illiterate majority of negroes in the State. The Constitution was at length agreed upon and was called the Constitution of 1895. This Constitution is the one under which we live today.

475. The Negro Schools. The negroes in South Carolina have a school system like that of the white people although they pay only a very small proportion of the taxes. After the slaves were freed so few of them were able to teach that many educated white men and women taught in the negro schools for a time. There are negro schools in every county in the state. The leading men of South Carolina since the War Between the Sections have urged that the negroes be given a common school education so as to make better citizens of them. The State partly supports a State College at Orangeburg for the negroes.

Finally, I include a photo from a family reunion. It occurred in 1954, shortly after the Supreme Court decision prohibiting segregated schools. The location is Summerton, SC, the site of Scotts Branch High School, the locus of our state's central role in the *Brown v. Board of Education* school desegregation case. I am among the four generations there, right up front among the kids, eighth from the right. I include the photo to complement an earlier point—the Simms text was likely imposed on everyone in the photo, along with about everyone else in the state.

Family Reunion, 1954
With permission of author

So, there we were, in the Sixties-South, South Carolinian in the sense of the WPA guide, steeped in Simms history and its spawn, and still faithful to the "Lost Cause." We were content with our "personal standards of right and wrong," and we preferred them to "those prescribed in courts of law." Contradictions abounded, but as further noted in the Guide, "woe to the outsider" who reminded us of them. Charitably characterized, we were stubborn, we were lazy thinkers, and we were prone to rage against perceived affronts to things South Carolinian, and we partied at Ocean Drive and Pawley's Island while historical opportunity passed us by.

Then the Vietnam War intervened, paradoxically. It drove some into antiwar factions and others to the hawks.

They were the outliers. Most remained somewhere in the middle, and I was right there with them, not eager to serve but reluctant to avoid it deliberately. For me, a sense of obligation to those of us who were already in the Asian jungles was powerful. Then, a trip to Fort Jackson for my pre-induction physical examination satisfied any appetite I had for military life, and later, I was both chagrined and relieved by the notice that I had flunked the exam. Even today, when my left knee asserts its personality, those old, complex emotions return, and they return at war memorials and when I recall those of us lost to the war.

Now, the Sixties are long gone, but we remain South Carolinian. We have new neighbors, new associates, and new colleagues, but we still love grits, prefer our tea sweet, our peanuts boiled[5], and our memories of the Sixties-South are mostly pleasant ones. Democrats are outliers.

Some of the old notions die hard, and their persistent vitality is evident. For example, consider our graceless response to suggestions (by outsiders?) that Tillman Hall might be renamed. Further, any thoughts of the "Cause" being finally "Lost" are unlikely to survive a visit to the web site of the South Carolina Sons of Confederate Veterans. There, an invitation to contribute to the erection of a monument commemorating the signers of the Ordinance of Secession is prominent.

Trying to understand the Sixties-South is not a new endeavor for me, and I know that I have evolved personally as my understanding of it has evolved. I realize this evolution starkly at gatherings of my old crowd, once parties and weddings, now more often funerals. Sometimes a country music refrain comes to mind, "I don't like half the folks I love,"[6] it goes.

---

[5] Boiled peanuts became the official SC State Snack in 2004. (SC Code § 1-1-682 (2024)

[6] Paul Thorn (Country Blues, Southern Rock musician), "I Don't Like Half the Folks I Love," (song inspired by a family reunion) 2010.

How the Governor's Mansion Got a Security Fence

Don Collins

When I think of the year 1968, I recall the Viet Cong's so-called Tet Offensive in Vietnam, the demonstrations at the Democratic Party's National Convention in Chicago, the antiwar movement, the civil rights and voting rights marches, the assassinations of Bobby Kennedy and Martin Luther King, and the urban riots that followed in Baltimore, Boston, Cleveland, Detroit, Pittsburgh, Washington, Raleigh, and Charlotte.

Raleigh and Charlotte were particularly troubling. I was in my final semester of a five-year-long professional degree program at North Carolina State University. I had signed up for an odd course, "Seminar on Ideas in Design." It was odd because it was only two credit hours; it was not required in my curriculum; it was taught by Henry Kamphoefner, the Dean of the College of Design; and it was taught in the living room of his home some distance from campus.

On the evening of April 4, 1968, I was in class sitting on the floor of Dean Kamphoefner's living room when his wife Mabel entered the room, walked over to his chair, leaned over and whispered into his ear. His face went pale, and he stared blankly as if seeing a foreboding future. Gaining his composure, he said, "Martin Luther King has been shot. I think it best to cancel tonight's class. Each of you, please go straight to your place of residence."

As I made my way the four or five miles back to my apartment, I thought I could see a distant glow in the sky in the direction of downtown Raleigh. It may have been my own paranoia unleashed by the moment. My thoughts quickly turned to my father, who was on his final night of duty before retirement as the Duty Officer at Charlotte Fire Department's Station 5 and Captain of Engine 5. As soon as I got to my apartment, I called my mother to let her know I was okay and to ask if she had heard from Dad. She had not. She said she had been calling the station every fifteen minutes to no avail. She was worried because the news channels were all saying there were numerous fires on the west side of Uptown. He was supposed to end his career at 8:00 AM the next day.

We did not hear from him until mid-morning. We later learned he and the crew members of Engine 5 and Ladder 5 were midway through his special retirement dinner at the station when the first alarm was struck. Finally returning home in the afternoon of the next day, he was exhausted, disappointed, and bitter over the outcome of his last night as a firefighter.

Everyone felt the tension of 1968. But people I knew rarely spoke directly about the situation.

But I also fondly recall a late-December 1968, late, late evening phone call, the consequence of which was somewhat related to the troubles of 1968. I did not know the caller or know how she got my phone number. She said she understood that I was a sculptor. I explained that I was a Landscape Architecture major at NCSU, and in my studies, I had taken three semesters of sculpture under Professor

Raymond Musslewhite. She asked if I had a sculpture piece, would I be willing to sell. She said she was looking for a unique Christmas gift. I said I had pieces that ranged in size from twelve inches to four feet, all made of old car bumper guards scrounged from a junk yard. I thought my description would turn her off, but she said she had already heard what they were made of, and they sounded fabulous. She asked if she could come look at my work the next evening after she got off work. I had to say, "Of course."

She arrived after dark. She looked at every piece thoroughly, asking how I arrived at the names I had given the pieces, what make of car the parts came from, how long the sculptures took to make, had they been in any art shows or galleries, etc. She finally picked a piece titled *The Walrus*. It was made of three bumper guards welded together and mounted to a torch-burnished eighteen-inch-long block of wood. The name was obvious when you looked at it.

We agreed on a purchase price, and she wrote me a check. But then she asked if I could deliver it to her at her office the next day. I replied that I was willing if her office was within a reasonable distance from Raleigh. She asked if I knew where the Governor's Mansion was in downtown Raleigh. I did; I had been by it a couple of times visiting some classmates who had a garage apartment nearby. The mansion was in the center of one of the four city-block-sized parks that made up the original plan of Raleigh—with one northeast of the Capitol, one southeast, one northwest, and one southwest. She said she was Governor Dan K. Moore's personal secretary. I asked for a time saying my afternoon studio class would not be over until 6:00. We agreed that I would deliver *The Walrus* about 6:30.

Just to be sure the deal was consummated, I cashed her check at my bank the next morning. By the time my afternoon class was over, it was raining—hard at times. I decided I had best wrap the piece to keep the rain off the wood base and to prevent any rust from forming. The wrap was done with brown butcher paper with *The Walrus* placed in a brown grocery bag. I did not want any possibility of the wet char on the base having a chance to mar any surface at the Governor's Mansion.

Heading to my car in the downpour, I opened the back door of my yellow-over-black '49 Chevrolet sedan delivery and tossed *The Walrus* inside onto the carpet. Now you must understand that the car I was driving was like a regular station wagon, but without windows on the side panels behind the front seats. Sedan deliveries were commonly used by florists and other merchants who had small parcels to deliver. I paid a whopping $67 for the vehicle when I purchased it in the summer of 1965 at a gas station a couple of blocks from where I worked as an intern at $1/hour. The $67 was my net pay for two weeks. I will leave it to the reader to imagine what kind of condition my $67 ride was in.

I knew where the Governor's Mansion was located, but I really did not know how to get to the Mansion proper but assumed I could figure it out. After all, I was a landscape architect-to-be and well versed in "reading the landscape." The landscape of Governor's Mansion Square had the house in the middle of the block in a grove of many trees and understory shrubs. At each corner, there was a driveway leading up to the side of the building. I drove around the block four times trying to decide which driveway was the main or correct one to use. They all looked to have the same magnitude of importance. "Just pick one," I said to myself. "Act like you own the place."

The driveway I picked led to a sally port on the side of the residence. I pulled under the shelter and shut off my engine, noting how dark it seemed. I tooted my horn. No one came out of the building. I tooted the horn again.

Nothing. The horn on this old car was not all that loud, and it could easily have been construed by someone in the residence as having come from the busy city streets that surrounded Mansion Square, I reasoned.

I also reasoned I was not going back home with *The Walrus*, so I got out of my car and grabbed the sculpture out of the back of the car. I noticed that in tossing the piece into the back of the delivery one of the pointed, projectile-shaped bumper guard pieces had torn through the brown paper wrap. Standing in the rain at the back of my vehicle, I was going to get soaked fixing the wrap. Too bad about the wrap, I concluded, for I was not going to ride home soaking wet in a car with only a so-so heater.

Mounting the steps to a small concrete porch under the cover of the sally port, I came to a door that was half glass and half wood. The upper glass panel was frosted. I knocked on the glass and waited. Nothing. I knocked again. Nothing. I knocked a third time, so hard the glass rattled. Nothing. Again, I thought to myself, "I am not taking the piece back home. It's been paid for."

I tried the door, and it was unlocked. I pushed it completely open. Down the long hallway a porter wearing a white smock leaned out of what looked like a phonebooth and shouted, "What you got in that bag?" I looked down at my wet grocery bag at the shiny tip of what looked like an artillery shell pointed down the hallway. I looked back up just in time to be confronted with three burly highway patrol officers and two plain clothes security officers, mere feet from me, who appeared out of nowhere.

In an instant, I was on my back on the ground between my car and the porch. I don't even know how I got there. I just remember flashlight beams in my face and shouts, "Who are you, what's in the bag, and what are you doing here?"

It took a few minutes for them to calm down. I tried
to explain I was instructed to deliver my sculpture to the
Governor's Mansion.

"By who," they demanded.

"By the Governor's personal secretary." I answered.

"What's her name," they asked, losing their patience.

"I don't know. I don't remember." In my haste to cash
her check, I had not made a mental note of her name. But,
lucky for me, the porter went to the secretary, and she was
able to call off security. They picked me up, brushed me off
as best they could, all the time scolding me for entering the
Governor's Mansion without permission.

Lesson learned. But the story does not end here.

For some time, I had been working part-time in the
office of Lewis Clarke and Associates while attending
North Carolina State. Lewis was a very talented landscape
architect well-known for his large-scale projects like
Palmetto Dunes on Hilton Head Island and the North
Carolina Zoo.

Lewis and his design office partner Charlie Burkhead
would hold a staff meeting every few weeks to review and
discuss potential projects being sought, new commissions,
and progress on current projects. At the first meeting
held after my episode at the Governor's Mansion,
Lewis announced that the firm had just been awarded a
commission to design a security and decorative wall around
the North Carolina Governor's Mansion.

So, the next time you are in Raleigh, take a trip around
the Governor's Mansion block and marvel at the wrought
iron and brick security fence and think to yourself, "I know
who is responsible for that fence being there—Don Collins
and all the other tension-creating events of the late Sixties."

North Carolina Execut ve Mansion, with fence

My hippie days in the Seventies

With permission of the author, Clementina Adams

The Hippie Years

Clementina E. Adams

The hippie movement was an exciting time that began in the U.S., in the mid-sixties, and lasted until the early 1970s. The movement then expanded to practically the entire world, including my country, Colombia. Initially, we saw the hippie movement through the media—not only in their way of dressing, but also in their love for their music, appreciation of nature, and an alternative lifestyle. "Hippie" was a common word in my country from the mid-Sixties to the early Seventies. We enjoyed looking at their eccentric tie-dye clothing and the flowery decorations the girls wore in their hair. We also enjoyed the music of a variety of bands and singers. It was as if a new and distinct perspective on the world was evolving before our eyes.

The hippie era had a limited but notable presence in Colombia, particularly in urban areas. We were aware of the hippies' musical festivals and ways of life. The music of the U.S. became a part of our music. We had house parties dressed as hippies, with colorful garments, lots of jewelry, and flowers in our hair. We became more in touch with nature and more expressive of our love for mutual interaction. During the Sixties and early Seventies, while not as widespread as in the United States or Europe, Colombian hippies embraced the values of peace, love, and alternative lifestyles, including sporadic communal living and, to a lesser extent, spiritual exploration through practices such as the use of psychedelic drugs; however, cannabis became more popular among youth.

Colombian hippies, like their counterparts around the world, rejected traditional values and institutions, including the established political and social order. The core values of the hippie movement, such as peace, love, and nonviolence, resonated among segments of Colombian society, especially among young people, who were searching for alternatives to the social conflicts and political instability in the country. Bogotá and other major cities in Colombia became centers for the hippie movement, where young people, inspired by the global counterculture, formed communities, shared ideas, and experimented with alternative ways of living. College students were one of the groups most interested in the new movement and felt motivated to embrace it.

While the hippie movement was dying in the U.S., in Colombia, we started to enjoy it, especially in our clothing and love for nature and peace. I remember some couples going to parks and getting lost in passionate embraces and kisses, but short of lovemaking in public. The only problem was that because of the theme "Make love, not war," there was a small group of daring married women who decided to cheat on their husbands for the sake of love.

In Colombia, the hippie movement didn't have a single end of era event, but rather a gradual decline beginning in the late Sixties. Several factors contributed to the end of the era, including violence associated with the movement, the mainstream adoption of some hippie ideals that became part of our culture, and the overall shift in the social and political landscapes.

The hippie movement also influenced art and culture in Colombia, with some artists and musicians incorporating countercultural themes and styles into their work. The tropical beach town of Palomino in the north of Colombia, a popular beach destination, is also known as one of the ultimate backpacker spots and hippie towns in Colombia.

In Colombia, the hippie movement is dead and the only way we remember that era is during carnival festivities that allow the population to dress in any style, including the psychedelic and colorful hippie looks in clothing, sashes, flowers in hair, beads, jewelry and other adornments. I still have pictures of my look during that time. My friends and I limited ourselves to being hippies in fashion only, due to our religious values and our upbringing. Currently, for Halloween and Mardi Gras in the U.S., and for carnival festival in Latin America, colorful hippie costumes can be purchased online for children and adults. It could be said that all around the world, there are people that have been influenced, affected, or at least intrigued by the hippie movement.

The Flower Child

Debra Broadwell Jackson

During my final two years in college, I enjoyed several exciting road trips with my classmates. We would drive six hours to Atlanta from Charleston, going the long way, from Charleston to Greenville to Atlanta. The I-20 interstate did not open until 1975, and we disliked back roads. These were the days before cells phones and FM radio in cars. My friend Cile had a portable, battery-operated 45 RPM record player and hundreds of 45 records. We could do an entire six-hour trip without repeating a song. The person who was lucky enough to sit in the front held the player, and we would pass records back and forth while singing. If you love Sixties beach music, you would have enjoyed the ride.

Atlanta was different from Charleston, and we were fascinated with the "hippies" who lived and played between 10th and 14th Streets and Peachtree Street. If you have spent any time in Atlanta, you may know there are numerous streets named Peachtree. But the crossroads in Midtown and Piedmont Park were brimming with young people day and night. We would drive by and look but avoided stopping or getting out of the car. A long line of cars was always driving by, watching the young and older people as they were singing, drinking, smoking pot, and just hanging out in the area.

At some point during these frequent road trips, Cile and I decided we wanted to work in Atlanta, and we made inquiries and applied for positions. We applied at Emory University Hospital and got interviews during one of our road trips. Emory provided us with written contracts for employment with a one-year commitment to the hospital.

In September 1971, Cile and I moved into our first Atlanta apartment, starting as staff nurses at Emory. Our friend, Shelia, would join us in December. We were paid once a month, and our annual salary was $8,770. I was glad I had roommates to share expenses. We were excited about starting work, renting a clean, new apartment, and living in a vibrant city. In 1972, I ventured into 14th Street area and saw George Carlin perform at a dive bar. A group of neighbors from my apartment complex planned the adventure. There was no one like Carlin at the time; he was crude, vulgar, offensive, and very funny. There were so few customers that after his show Carlin joined our table for drinks. Off stage he was okay, but I still would not pay to see him again.

It would take several years, but eventually I met and became friends with several "Flower Children." They had earned an undergraduate degree or at least attended college. Their lifestyles were different from mine. They did not want to "own" anything. They were disturbed I was buying a house, since being weighed down by anything material was inconceivable to them. Almost all worked waiting on tables at high-end restaurants and earned more in tips each week than I did in my full-time position. They were unconcerned about health insurance or retirement programs. I worked forty hours a week; they worked twenty five. While I was working, they were sleeping.

They shared their beliefs with me and told me what they wanted out of life. They told me about EST, transcendental meditation, the Silva Doctrine, the Rosicrucian Order, Scientology, even crystals. Each offered new techniques for relaxation, stress reduction, and personal reflection. And I did try some of them. In the late seventies, the group moved to Clayton, Georgia, and set up a commune. I visited them there once and was so happy to see them. A close friend, Susie, now had a son, a five-year old who ran up to us calling out, "Mamma, Mamma, tit, tit." I was stunned that he was still breastfeeding. I was not impressed, but they seemed very happy.

Susie's dog gave birth to my first golden retriever, Heather, which brought much joy to me. She was a great pet and lived a long and happy life in our home, which became filled full of stuff and things in Atlanta. I was grateful to be exposed to the lifestyles and interests of the flower children, but my acceptance of responsibility and traditional lifestyles was certainly no chore for me. The weight felt right.

Farewells, August 1974

Susan Hilligoss

"Where does this go?" Someone was holding a
pitcher of tea and needed a spot for it on the
long table set up in the backyard. Someone else scooted
paper plates and napkins out of the way. The charcoal
grill was going. It was going to be a fun farewell picnic.
I was relieved. This was my house, well, the house in a
Philadelphia suburb where I lived with a half dozen other
young people, including my boyfriend. We were used
to having one or two extras at dinner any time. But this
evening I was hosting a group of women, and after dinner
we were all looking forward to watching television later.

The day Richard Nixon resigned the presidency of the
United States was also the last day of my women's self-
defense class. I cannot think of one without the other.
Nixon's time in the White House, from his war policies to
the Watergate scandal, had horrified me, so the class, which
I took every semester including summers for two years on
Penn's campus, had sustained me through national political
turmoil as well as personal doldrums while I toiled in
graduate school.

The two came together on August 8, 1974, a Thursday.
We had our usual 5:00 p.m. class—calisthenics, then
punching and kicking exercises and some sparring in a

little-used dance studio with a mirror to check our form.
From the ceiling there hung a long, heavy bag for kicking.
You hit it with your closed fist only if you dared—it was
so hard. The oldest student, a biologist whose hair was
graying, had no problem punching that bag as hard as she
could. She said she imagined her department chairman's
face on it every time. We all had personal stories of gender
bias at the university, and some had worse tales. These
were only alluded to with pursed lips and shoulder shrugs,
as culture far outweighed the law regarding discrimination
and abuse.

The weather was nice that late summer day, so we may
have run a few laps barefoot around the rubberized track at
Penn's rickety football stadium, which was adjacent to the
gym with the dance studio. We were only yards from the
Schuylkill River that divides West Philadelphia from Center
City. After class, we dressed. We sometimes headed out as
a group, on foot, in a couple of cars, or on public transit,
to a cheap eatery, usually ethnic—Chinese, Italian, or even
a kosher dairy restaurant. I cherished these classes, the
routine, the camaraderie with women across campus. This
time we headed west toward Lansdowne, the crowded little
suburb where I lived.

Everyone loved our instructor, who had started the class
a couple of years before. Most of us just took the course
over and over. Gloria was a committed feminist, a former
doctoral student in sociology, now a law student. She had
a brown belt in Shotokan, a Japanese form of karate. Her
dojo, the Eastern Karate Association, located in a prominent
storefront over on the west side of campus, had thrown her
out for teaching martial arts. Brown belts were not allowed
to teach. But no woman had ever achieved a black belt
there, and as far as anyone knew, no woman ever would.
Gloria didn't care. She persuaded the university to offer
the recreational class with the generic title "women's self-

defense," and when she taught, she wore her white gi, but no belt, both out of respect to her teachers, and as a protest.

Now Gloria was leaving to go to Waycross, Georgia, to be a public defender. The picnic was mainly a farewell dinner for Gloria and thus an end to the class, but that evening was also Nixon's farewell to public office. For two years, the Watergate scandal had galvanized me, my friends, and certainly the women present that night. It was widely thought that after the "smoking gun" tape transcript had been published on August 5, Nixon would have to resign. I had volunteered to host on the 8th because our house was plenty large enough for this group, with a big dining room, a backyard, and a television. Everyone anticipated that he would address the public that evening.

The picnic was hastily planned and no one brought much of anything—schlepping groceries from the food-desert that was West Philly was not an option. I think we had hot dogs and burgers, hoping the vegetarians could cope. Our house always had lots of beer—it was cheaper than milk in German-influenced Pennsylvania. No doubt we had a couple of Entenmann's, which was Philly-speak for boxes of local baked goods, which could range from breakfast pastries to pound cakes, and which were available at every WaWa, the convenience store chain. Coffee was in the house as well. I don't remember much talking while we ate. We had a speech to watch.

Then everyone settled into the big living room, on couches and soft chairs, but mainly on the floor, to watch the little color TV set up at one end. The other residents of the house came in too, so there were maybe fourteen or fifteen of us. I stood for a while in the hall at the entrance, just watching their rapt faces, the only light, the only sounds, coming from the TV screen. I steeled myself for the all too familiar face on the television, yet I was stunned by the words and the historic moment. It was everything we had yearned for and more, yet there was no chatter. No cheers or laughter. I don't recall people leaving or saying goodbye to sparring partners I would never see again, just that tableau.

The absurdist in me laughs, or grimaces, at the bizarre rationale for the get together, but I am still awed by being there at that time with those particular others. My frame does not center the famous high forehead, that blankly earnest face of scandal. My frame centers that house, those faces intent on the screen. I think now: These were my people, and this was how we did things.

Summer of Judgment

Victoria Ridgeway Gillis

In the summer of 1973, I was a junior high school science teacher with five years' experience in the South, recently relocated to the Orlando area. I was refinishing an antique iron bed, repainting with enough coats of paint to ward off rusting. We had a small TV, which I repositioned in the garage, and as I painted, I watched the televised hearings. There was nothing else on—my soap operas were superseded by a parade of witnesses who initially were, quite frankly, boring. I didn't really care about the organization of CREEP (The Committee to Re-Elect the President) though as I listened, I thought how aptly the group had been named. As the parade of witnesses continued and John Dean took the stand, the testimony became riveting. I gave my life over to the Senate Watergate Hearings that summer.

I remember Dean's dull monotone that would have otherwise put me to sleep . . . but he was saying the most unbelievable things. Unbelievable unless you were also watching the news each night, seeing President Nixon reveal himself slowly through his actions against the news media and his ranting about the Pentagon Papers.

The Pentagon Papers hit me particularly hard because I had completed my undergraduate degree at a small military college, North Georgia College (NGC), in Dahlonega. Dahlonega was so isolated that from 1964 to 1967 I was oblivious to the increasing public outcry against the Vietnam War. Another reason for ignorance was that my male classmates were in a rigorous ROTC program, compulsory at NGC, the only coeducational military college in the nation at that time. We had Saturday morning classes because the male students engaged in war games on Wednesday mornings, when classes were suspended. Most of them shipped out to Vietnam as their first posting. By the summer of 1973 I had lost three of my best friends from college to that war along with nine other classmates. At 27, a number of my college friends were widows.

All that summer, I obsessively watched the hearings. I remember the spine-tingling I felt when Alexander Butterfield, whom I did not know existed before the day he testified about a Presidential taping system, dropped the penny that began rolling to the unavoidable end. I remember the heavy feeling deep in my chest that made it difficult to breathe as each days' news painted a darker picture of a President that had ridden into re-election on a wave of jubilant expectations. Most Americans had voted for Nixon; now a flood of telegrams (the 1970s version of text messages) was inundating Congress with a singular message: Impeach Nixon.

By August of 1974, along with the rest of the nation, I was waiting uncertainly for the conclusion. It was a strange feeling that evening, watching a President resign from office—a mixture of relief with an undercurrent of anxiety for what came next. That summer hooked me on politics, and I remain an addict to this day.

Contributors

Clementina E. Adams

Then   Now

I was born in Barranquilla, Colombia, South America,
where I received a Licentiate (MA) in Hispanic
American Culture and Literature. Through the Organization
of American States, I earned two scholarships, 1973-1974
for an MS in Instructional Design and Development, and
another in 1976-78 for a PhD in Instructional Systems,
both at Florida State University, Tallahassee, Florida. I
taught Spanish at Gallaudet University, Washington, DC
and at the University of Alaska-Fairbanks. I worked at
the State Department of Education, Columbia, SC, 1985-
1989. I came to Clemson University in 1989 as a faculty
member in the Languages Department. I have published
three books and over forty articles in refereed and peer-
reviewed journals. I pioneered projects and programs in

my Department such as coordinating Foreign Languages for Elementary School Children (FLES), the inclusion of American Sign Language (ASL) as part of the Department offerings, and the development of a new major, Language and International Health (L&IH). I led service-learning activities for improving the life of the Hispanic community in the Upstate. I have received honors and awards at the regional, national, and international levels. In 2004 and in 2006, I received the CU Award for Faculty Excellence, the CU Service Alliance Faculty Fellow Award, 2008-2009 and 2011-2012. I became a member of the Emeritus College in 2014. In 2015, I was certified as a Spanish Interpreter by the Certification Commission for Healthcare Interpreters (CCHI). In 2020 I was inducted into the College of Architecture, Arts, and Humanities Hall of Fame. I have continued to publish and participate in activities through the Emeritus College at CU.

Chris Benson

Then   Now

Chris Benson was a research associate and a senior lecturer of British literature and advanced writing at Clemson University from 1990—2002 and from 2007—2020. He was publications coordinator for the Bread Loaf Teacher Network from 1993 to 2002 and published the semiannual *Bread Loaf Teacher Magazine*, which contains classroom articles, action research reports, book reviews, interviews, and stories written by and for teachers. Issues of the magazine reported on writing for the community, teacher research, school reform, networked learning, learning technology, community building, teaching in rural communities, and educational policy.

He is retired from academia and spends his time performing music with various bands, including bluegrass, old time, Americana, and Sixties and Seventies pop. He also spends time gardening and canning and writing stories and poems. His books have been published by Teacher College Press, Heinemann Publishing, Chapbooks for Learning, and the Institute on Family and Neighborhood Life.

Don Collins

Then

Now

A native of Charlotte, NC, Don Collins began his academic journey via Furman University while on active military duty with the USAF. Completing his military obligation, he enrolled at Clemson University (CU) to study in the College of Architecture. After witnessing a presentation by a landscape architect guest speaker, Don transferred to North Carolina State University (NCSU), where he completed the five-year professional degree, Bachelor of Landscape Architecture, in 1968.

While at NCSU, he worked for four different Landscape Architectural firms. In the summer following his fourth year of study, on a flight back from presenting plans for a new college campus, his employer suggested he apply for graduate school at Harvard. Don took his advice, applied to Harvard and was accepted. Having a five-year undergraduate degree, Don, completed the Master of Landscape Architecture degree, graduating in 1969.

After Harvard, Don accepted a faculty position at Ball State University's (BSU) College of Architecture and Planning. BSU's dean had been his first-year design studio professor at Clemson University (CU). Don remained at BSU for three years before accepting a position in Architectural Studies at CU's College of Architecture for the fall of 1972. While at BSU, an architectural niche seed was planted that would eventually redefine his academic focus.

In 1977, the Dean of Architecture, recalling a fire station among Don's work at BSU, summoned Don to his office. Acting on a charge from the university's president, the dean asked him to work with a nearby volunteer fire department on a design for a station to be built on university property. Don engaged his students in the effort. The CU fire chief was invited to the reviews of the student work. Impressed, the fire chief invited Don to work with the CUFD. The dean agreed, changing two legs of Don's "three-legged stool." "Public Service" was changed to his work with the CUFD and the "Research" leg to focus on architecture and the fire service. That soon became fire stations. Don has visited of over 300 stations for "post-occupancy" evaluations.

In 1995, Don was appointed Head of the newly created Department of Planning and Landscape Architecture, a position he held until 2003. Don retired from CU in 2005 and is now busying himself as a fire station design consultant. He has been engaged in over thirty projects in the U.S. and Canada.

Marty Duckenfield

Then

Now

Our family moved to Hartsdale, one of the multiple small villages located along the commuter rail service to New York City, in 1950, and it was there, the third of four children, I grew up from kindergarten onwards. Our family was strongly linked to a school, church, and community life that sheltered us from much of the outside world and nurtured us with values that have lasted a lifetime.

Once I graduated in 1960 from Hartsdale Junior High in a class of 63 students, my classmates and I boarded a bus to nearby White Plains High School. Going to this high school of 2,300 students provided us with new opportunities and greater diversity. My parents expected all of us to both attend college and work summers from the age of 16 to earn money to help pay those college fees. My job was working five summers in an insurance company in lower Manhattan, rating auto insurance policies.

I attended college in Maine and studied abroad in Oxford in 1965-6 for my junior year. Upon graduation, I became a seventh-grade teacher of language arts and social studies in a rural area of Connecticut before returning to England with my British husband to live and start our family. His career in mathematics and computers eventually led us back to the U.S. where he taught at a college in Ohio for five years. I volunteered in a wide range of activities there before we moved south. I attended graduate school at Clemson, earning a master's degree in nutrition, aiming for a career based on my values of service to others, learned while growing up in Hartsdale.

At Clemson University, after two years of teaching in elementary schools, I began working in 1988 at the National Dropout Prevention Center for 25 years, training educators through national and regional workshops, publications, and web-based educational learning with a focus on service learning. From 2013-2018, I spent my final five years producing video content on educational improvement with Clemson Broadcast Productions.

Victoria Ridgeway Gillis

Then   Now

I was born in 1946 and grew up in a small town near
Atlanta, Lithonia. My mother's family lived there, and
I enjoyed growing up with numerous cousins, aunts, and
uncles, and eventually three siblings. My childhood was
spent playing outside as there was no air conditioning
in those days. There was a whole "gang" of us kids who
grew up in that small, sun-drenched town. We rode our
bikes, skated, and played various games until time to go
home, about thirty minutes after twilight, known to us as
"dark-thirty." I went to school in the building in which
my grandmother, her siblings, and my mother had gone to
school. We had a teacherage on the grounds of the school
along with a house for the principal, both relics left from a
time when Lithonia had an independent school system. In

1962, in the middle of my sophomore year in high school, my father died, and my childhood was over.

After graduating high school, I chose North Georgia College (NGC), the military college in Georgia because my father had graduated from there. I intended to teach high school biology, which ironically is the only science course I never taught.

I taught science in the K-12 school system for twenty years before completing my graduate studies and heading to a career in higher education. After twenty years at Clemson University, I retired in 2010 as a Professor Emerita of Literacy. Then I accepted a position at the University of Wyoming as an Endowed Excellence Chair in literacy education. In this collection of stories, you will read my personal memoirs that span the entirety of the long decade of the Sixties. My view of the Sixties is not that of a teenager during those tumultuous years, though I was that age, but of a young woman struggling to survive. Those struggles have stood me in good stead. I look back on my life and wonder at the fabulous things I have been privileged to experience. I am so richly blessed.

Susan Hilligoss

| Then | Now |

I grew up in a small town in Indiana. For me life in the Sixties was a series of moves. In 1960, my family moved to a small town in Michigan. I was twelve. In 1965 we moved back to Indiana, this time to Indianapolis. I returned north to the University of Michigan for college, spending summers in Indianapolis, where I worked at several jobs. For almost the entire decade of the Seventies I lived in or near Philadelphia, where I attended graduate school at the University of Pennsylvania and later taught English at a branch campus of Pennsylvania State University and Bryn Mawr College. So, for me, the "Where were you when" questions about cataclysmic events during the "long decade" of this volume call to mind a patchwork of backdrops in three states. There were television accounts, of course, but the shocking news actually reached me in other ways, in sleepy high school and college libraries; in a massive government installation; and at an impromptu picnic and watch party. During this span, I matured from a child into an adult, experiencing these historical moments differently as I grew, sharing them with an ever-widening group of people, and learning (I hope) to ponder the deep questions these events raised. In 1979 I moved south, at first to teach at the University of North Carolina at Charlotte and then, in 1983, Clemson University. I retired in 2014 and still live in Clemson.

Cecil Huey

Then

Now

My boyhood home is about twenty miles from Clemson. I belong to The Anderson Boys High School Class of 1961, the next-to last class from the old racially segregated, single-gender school. Having shown a little high school athletic promise, I arrived on the Clemson campus with the welcome benefits of a track and field scholarship.

I had been fairly good at math, science, and tinkering, prompting some to suggest that I might turn out to be an engineer. I guessed they might have been right and enrolled in Mechanical Engineering. At this remove, I recall few aspirations beyond the hope of not disappointing my folks.

Upon graduation, graduate school, and the rest, I passed a few years in South Louisiana and South Georgia before joining the Clemson faculty in 1975.

Recently, an old friend summed me up to a newcomer as once a skinny, dark-haired kid with thick glasses, a member of the track team, and then a long-time Clemson professor. I still wear glasses.

He continued, adding a few things beyond the usual academic boilerplate. He mentioned my having thumbed across the country along with a friend, my years-long involvement in athletics, and my seven-year stint on the South Carolina State Board of Registration for Professional Engineers and Surveyors. The hitchhiking afforded my first view of the inside of a squad car, prompted musings of the sort born of late-night exhaustion along desert highways in the dusty wash of passing cars, and it illuminated some unromantic elements of US 66.

My thirteen years as Clemson's Faculty Athletics Representative and the State Board stretch taught the elusiveness of reason, the necessity of diplomacy and the envy of Solomon. I learned by teaching, and I think of myself as an educator. I retired in 2006.

Debra Broadwell Jackson

Then[1]   Now

My formative years were spent growing up in the sixties in Anderson, SC I left at seventeen to move to the big city of Charleston for college and to the real big city of Atlanta for employment. I am a nurse. No matter how many degrees or disciplines I have studied, I am a nurse. The people with whom I worked and for whom I cared were my teachers. My perspectives and understanding of the issues of this extended timeframe of unrest and social change provided opportunities I had never envisioned. I never considered myself a "feminist" and yet I was. My dad loved to say, "if I had a child in jail and one in Georgia, I would get the one out of Georgia first." So, I

---

[1] Debbie Jackson, photo from the Caducean, 1971, page 102, Courtesy of the Waring Historical Library, MUSC, Charleston, SC

bought a house in a downtown Atlanta neighborhood. He never understood the draw of the city, the excitement of working at a major medical research university, meeting and working with colleagues to make changes in patient care and education.

After nineteen years at Emory University as a staff nurse, nurse clinician, director of a non-degree nursing program, and finally a tenured associate professor of nursing, I had opportunities to publish, conduct research, serve as a president of a specialty nursing organization, travel across 48 of the 50 states and internationally. In November 1990, I took a big step with Vince, my husband. Twenty-three years and two babies later, I returned to upstate South Carolina and to Clemson to see what would happen next.

The "next" was 26 years at Clemson University as a professor and department chair, interim dean of the graduate school, and finally assistant to the president and associate provost. The best position came after retirement, when I was selected as the director of Clemson's Emeritus College.

Kenneth Steven Marsh

Then   Now

The Sixties were formative years for me. I worked at a sports car dealer to earn money to extend a trip to visit my uncle in Geneva, Switzerland, and took on extra responsibilities when I saw my inebriated boss asleep at his desk when a customer came in. I took my first trip on a new jet plane at age seventeen and spent two days in London on my own before proceeding to Switzerland. I returned home with my uncle's family on the SS France. Uncle Ben worked for the United Nations, so I visited the Geneva and N.Y. headquarters (including the delegates lounge) that influenced activities decades later. I began political action with the March on Washington in 1963 and joined political campaigns including that for our congressional representative who was later assassinated.

My formative years also included professional training. I entered Adelphi University intent on being a physics major. Since freshman register last, I was closed out of first-semester of physics that was the prerequisite for the second semester. I ended up graduating as an undecided major with almost twice the credits required for a chemistry major, one course shy of physics major, and two courses shy of a math major. That put me in good stead for the future—but I still had to fight the draft.

Jim Palmer

Then

Now

Jim Palmer spent the Sixties in college. From 1960–64, still living on the family farm in Anderson County, he commuted to Clemson as an undergraduate. At Clemson, Jim worked as student assistant to Professor Wilbert Byrd. Jim earned his BS from Clemson in 1964 and continued his education at the University of Georgia where he earned a master's degree in plant genetics in 1966.

Returning to Clemson for his PhD, Jim worked again with Professor Byrd, who was by then the head of the Department of Experimental Statistics. In 1969, after defending his dissertation in Plant Genetics, Jim, then 27 years of age, was reclassified 1-A by the draft board, and received notice to report to Fort Jackson. His lottery number was 32. He thought he was going to Vietnam for sure.

But he didn't.

President Nixon had just ordered that 26 was the cutoff age for the draft. With great relief, Jim took a job in 1970 at Clemson Univesrity as Extension Soybean Specialist and Assistant Professor of Agronomy and Soils with joint teaching and research responsibilities.

Jim's research at Clemson, included cropping systems for sustaining profitability. The American Soybean Association included Jim on a national soybean research tour and study missions to England, Germany and South America.

He was recognized for his work with a Life Membership Award from the American Soybean Association. He received a Public Service Award from the Clemson Alumni Association, and in 1993 the *Progressive Farmer* magazine named him "Man of the Year" for service to South Carolina agriculture.

In 1970, he married Kate Salley, from Orangeburg, SC. They have two children and two grandchildren.

Rosanne Pruitt

Then   Now

Rosanne Harkey Pruitt spent the Sixties attending grammar school and high school, graduating in 1970. She moved multiple times, arriving in the Upstate in 1967. A graduate of Emory University and the University of South Carolina, Rosanne taught at Clemson briefly then moved to Maryland with her family to obtain a PhD. Rosanne served as Director of the School of Nursing at Clemson University and retired as Professor Emerita in 2018 to care for family members. While at Clemson, Rosanne led the development of the Nurse Practitioner graduate programs and while Director helped to launch the interdisciplinary PhD in Healthcare Genetics. Her scholarly grants and publications are in health promotion and evaluation. She currently serves as the Emeritus College representative on the Well Being Council.

In retirement, Rosanne, a family nurse practitioner, volunteers weekly at the Anderson Free Clinic. She is a Master Gardener and enjoys working in her yard. She is active in her church as a volunteer and a teaching elder. She enjoys tennis, yoga, walking and spending time with family, including grandchildren, age one and almost three.

Dolores (Dee) Stegelin

Then

Now

Growing up on a dairy farm in north central Kansas, my perspective on the Sixties and Seventies was from a more sheltered and rural perspective. During this formative period in my life, I attended a small rural school with fewer than twenty students and then a consolidated high school with about 500 students. My childhood was filled with many exploratory outdoor experiences and chores on the farm, 4-H, church, and community activities, and a love for learning and all things "school." During my high school years in the early Sixties, I lost my father to cancer, left home for the first time to attend Kansas State University, navigated a full-time academic course schedule while working full-time, and prepared myself for adulthood. In this period of ten years, the transition from childhood to adulthood came quickly and painfully. Situated within this already heavy decade for me personally were the assassinations of three very important people— JFK, RFK, and Dr. King—and the direct experiences of the Vietnam War. It was a lot to confront, deal with, learn and heal from. To me, the Sixties were a series of traumatic experiences and a tough introduction to a world that seemed much more complex than a dairy farm. The Seventies proved to be challenging also, and many of those events stemmed from the events of the Sixties. I am proud of my life accomplishments, and I share this writing with you as a professor emerita at Clemson University in the field of early childhood education. I am grateful for the Emeritus College and the Memoir Writing Group.

Stephen H. Wainscott

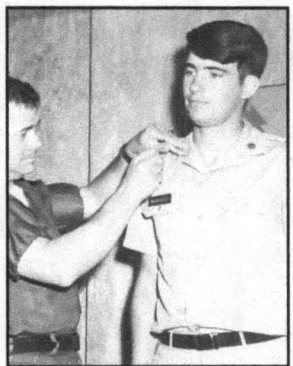 

Then   Now

In 1952 my family moved to Charlotte from Chadds Ford, PA. At the age of six, I had never seen an African American person before. All I knew was that they were called (in polite circles, at least) Negroes. It was not until I reached my teenage years that I came face to face with the cruel reality of segregation and the myth of "separate but equal." After coming to the political science department at Clemson, I did research on the phenomenon of "second-generation discrimination," meaning practices of segregating Black students within schools that appeared to be integrated. I can't help but think that my research was sparked in part by my adolescent encounters with injustice. The issue of justice would surface again, albeit in a different way, in 1969 when I was faced with a conflict between loyalty to my country and my growing opposition to the war in Vietnam. At first, I entertained the thought of fleeing to Canada. In the end, I enlisted in the Army and rode out the war as an intelligence officer at Ft. Bragg, N.C. There have been other "teachable moments" in my life, but my encounters with racial injustice and the moral dilemma I faced with my decision to bear arms were the most impactful.

Acknowledgments

The able and enthusiastic assistance of Victoria Muscheff, our Emeritus College Program Coordinator, the Photoshop wizardry of Professor Emeritus Sam Wang, the able design assistance of Professor Emeritus John Leininger, and the patient and insightful design and editing services of Christine Prado are greatly appreciated.

Editing team

Chris Benson, Marty Duckenfield, Susan Hilligoss, Cecil Huey, Debra Jackson

Contributors, pictured back cover

Left to right:
Steve Wainscott, Cecil Huey, Debra Jackson,
Dee Steglin, Susan Hilligoss, Clementina Adams,
Roseanne Pruitt, Vicki Gillis, Chris Benson,
Marty Duckenfield, Ken Marsh, Jim Palmer
Missing from the photo: Don Collins